Dear Jenn

As you get used [to being]
1st in your ministry while
adjusting to having a two
year old ☺ I pray that
when hard

In His Everlasting Arms

& moments arise
these pages encourage.

Gail
9/26/14

In His Everlasting Arms

৵

Learning to Trust God in All Circumstances

Gail MacDonald

Gail MacDonald

Ps. 62:1-2

Regal

From Gospel Light
Ventura, California, U.S.A.

PUBLISHED BY REGAL BOOKS
FROM GOSPEL LIGHT
VENTURA, CALIFORNIA, U.S.A.
PRINTED IN THE U.S.A.

Regal Books is a ministry of Gospel Light, a Christian publisher dedicated to serving the local church. We believe God's vision for Gospel Light is to provide church leaders with biblical, user-friendly materials that will help them evangelize, disciple and minister to children, youth and families.

It is our prayer that this Regal book will help you discover biblical truth for your own life and help you meet the needs of others. May God richly bless you.

For a free catalog of resources from Regal Books/Gospel Light, please call your Christian supplier or contact us at 1-800-4-GOSPEL *or* www.regalbooks.com.

Originally published by Servant Publications in 2000.

The publisher thanks Christian Literature Crusade (CLC) for permission to reprint excerpts from *Rose From Brier, Toward Jerusalem, and Whispers of His Power*. All rights reserved.

Portions of this book have been adapted from *A Step Farther and Higher*, by Gail MacDonald (Sisters, Ore.: Multnomah, 1989).

Cover design by Paul Higdon
Cover art "He Shall Hear My Voice." © C. Michael Dudash, used by permission from DaySpring® Cards, The MasterPeace® Collection, all rights reserved. For further information about this and other works by C. Michael Dudash, contact The MasterPeace Collection at 1-800-944-8000.

**Library of Congress Cataloging-in-Publication Data
(Applied for)**

ISBN: 0-8307-3447-3

1   2   3   4   5   6   7   8   9   10   11   12   13   14   15   /   09   08   07   06   05   04

Rights for publishing this book in other languages are contracted by Gospel Light Worldwide, the international nonprofit ministry of Gospel Light. Gospel Light Worldwide also provides publishing and technical assistance to international publishers dedicated to producing Sunday School and Vacation Bible School curricula and books in the languages of the world. For additional information, visit www.gospellightworldwide.org; write to Gospel Light Worldwide, P.O. Box 3875, Ventura, CA 93006; or send an e-mail to info@gospellightworldwide.org.

Dedication

๕๖

Over the years, I've come to realize that *knowing* we are in his everlasting arms depends on those who care enough to cover us in daily prayer. Without them, we wouldn't want to make plans, venture out, say a word. Gordon and I *know* that if God's power doesn't rest on us in response to prayer, we might as well hang it up. I'm thankful for the untold hours of love that can be valued only in heaven's economy. It brings joy to me to dedicate this book to:

Our children: Mark and Patty MacDonald and Kristy and Tom McLaughlin

And to our "prayer covering": Joanna Mockler, Lourine Clark, Janet Avery, Lois Wells, Keith and Judy Fredrickson, Doug and Bev Nelson, Frances Madison, Alice Pinard, Karen Mains, Donna MacLoed, Charlotte Demetri, Betsy Ryder, Lois Farrell, Lena Napalitano, Jean Merrill, Pat Spaziani, Susan Shaeffer, Judy Long, and Nan McCullough.

Contents

ૐ

Acknowledgments

To our daughter Kristy, and my dear friend Joanna: My unbounded thankfulness for the gifts of your precious time, wisdom, and insight as you lovingly combed this book in order to make it more readable. I treasure your "second-mile" support.

My gratitude also for the eager encouragement my editor, Heidi Hess Saxton, has given to me. You are not only a competent author in your own right, Heidi, but have the God-given ability to spur on writers like myself by "seeing" a good book before it is! Thank you for never being too busy to lend your time and expertise.

And to Gordon, my husband of nearly forty years. I wouldn't even have begun such a venture without your love-nudge, cheerleading, and attentive care to the minutest nuances in this manuscript. Your steadied soul is my daily picture of one who leans on arms that are eternal. As with each volume that we finish, this is *our* work.

Introduction

Have you ever noticed the expression of an infant being carried on the shoulder of his mother or father? The baby's face is a study in total relaxation. While the parent sees where the two are headed, the child can see only where they have been. He knows this is a place of safety and protection.

I can recall numerous people who have found such trust in God during times of great unrest in their lives. They couldn't see where they were going, either, but they had learned to trust God *before* this. For instance, I remember a woman in her late forties who had cancer throughout her body. Whenever I was with her, I came away inspired to trust God more. She was fine, she said, "Don't worry about me, God is meeting me in amazing ways and I'm resting in his care." Not once, but many times, the same conversation took place. God's everlasting arms were holding her. Period. Her ability to take hold of this certainty made it far easier for her daughter, who was in college, to cope and find her strength in God as well.

Ever since the beginning of biblical history, the arm of God has been reaching out to his loved creation. Moses reminded his people of this:

Ask now about the former days, long before your time, from the day God created man on the earth; ask from one end of the heavens to the other. Has anything so great as this ever happened, or has anything like it ever been heard of?... Has any god ever tried to take for himself one nation out of another nation, by testings, by miraculous signs and wonders, by war, by a mighty hand and an outstretched arm, or by great and awesome deeds, like all the things the Lord your God did for you in Egypt before your very eyes?

DEUTERONOMY 4:32,34

Over and over, they saw in the hand and arm of God a promise of provision and protection. God told them how he would do it: "I will redeem you with an outstretched arm and mighty acts of judgment. I will take you as my own people, and I will be your God" (Ex 6:6-7). These are words of belonging. Then and now, we need to know that we are God's very own children, and his loving care for us will be eternal. Claim this...

Just before he died, Moses spoke final words of consolation: "The eternal God is your refuge, and underneath are the everlasting arms" (Dt 33:27). As I studied "the arm of God" throughout the Older Testament, I found it to be a thread throughout the whole.

This was no weak arm, but a powerful and mighty one. It takes great strength for One so strong to show gentleness. It is to this that I would like to focus our thoughts.

Is there any more beautiful picture of this than the one Isaiah gave us? "He gathers the lambs in his arms and carries them close to his heart." (Is 40:11) Did we not see this in the life of Jesus, our Lord, when it was said of him, "He took the children in his arms, put his hands on them and blessed them" (Mk 10:16)?

This is no academic subject for me. Gordon, my husband, and I have known what it is like to be upheld by these everlasting arms. Those arms have been instantly available to us when we have been in the crucible of life's experiences. It's hard to express to others what it's like; <u>you simply know that *someone* is</u> THIS <u>holding you up when everything inside of you feels like giving</u> <u>way.</u>

In this book, you will read of many others for whom these arms have been enough. God's gentle, outstretched, everlasting ₽S 4ₒ arms are *still* our refuge and strength, a present help in time of need. As you read on, embrace the joy of knowing this *can* be a reality for your life in this day and forever.

Gail MacDonald
Canterbury, New Hampshire

Section One
❧
A Look at the Heart of God

must understand God's character to fully trust in Him

Until we have a correct understanding of God's character, trusting him is difficult and our faith journey flounders. As you read this first section, I hope your heart will be fine-tuned to God's love, control, grace, truth, majesty, power, and forgiveness. May you have an even deeper understanding of how much your heavenly Father longs to communicate intimately with you.

In times when we are shattered by life's crises, our understanding of God's love may be challenged. As I reflect on the dark times in my life, I see how *knowing* for certain that God is always good, always present, no matter the circumstances, helped me to cope.

Does the God you follow listen, respond, and come to you with strength and compassion? As we choose to look beyond our immediate circumstances to see the arms of our loving God who sustains us, we will come to experience his love far more deeply than we ever dreamed possible.

That is such a hard choice

> Your faithfulness continues through all generations;
>   you established the earth, and it endures.
> Your laws endure to this day,
>   for all things serve you.

PSALM 119:90-91

How?! How do I look beyond this? My ♡ is broken... I am broken... So much loss in such a short time...

I am trying to find the joy in this that... ↓

I appear to have it all together on the outside but inside I am broken & hurt & confused & angry... I know I have never met this baby... but I've seen it and have loved it for 3 months. This was my rainbow baby. I'm having a hard time with the why. And I know it's not for me to question or know... I'm struggling → Father, no one but you knows how much...

One

Trusting in God's Unseen Hand

> "For my thoughts are not your thoughts, neither are your ways my ways," declares the Lord. "As the heavens are higher than the earth, so are my ways higher than your ways and my thoughts than your thoughts."
>
> ISAIAH 55:8-9

When I was first learning to follow Christ, I didn't have a living spiritual mentor. I did have numerous dead ones, though—in books. They have been and are my friends. Through them I have been treated to a glimpse of the heart of God.

One such "friend" is Amy Carmichael—her lofty view of God has invited me to stretch spiritually. This was a woman who *knew* what it meant to rest in God's everlasting arms. Amy spent over fifty years of her life in India, where she founded and directed a fellowship for children in moral danger. Hundreds of children passed through this "safe" place.

After laboring in this fashion for over thirty years, Amy was in a serious accident; the final twenty years of her life were spent in bed. From there she superintended the day-to-day operation of the Dohnavur Fellowship, and from there she wrote her richest books. Amy cautioned people not to play "if-only" games as they recalled the night of her injury. In fact, her wounds could have been much worse: The lorry that drove her forty-six miles to the hospital nearly fell into a ravine due to bad weather. Once she reflected on the accident in this way:

> If [the ambulance] had gone over, would we say prayer was unanswered? It is a petty view of our Father's love and wisdom which demands or expects an answer according to our demand, apart from his wisdom.
>
> We see hardly one inch of the narrow lane of time. To our God eternity lies open as a meadow. It must seem strange to the heavenly family who have seen the beautiful end of the Lord, that we should ever question what love allows to be, or ever call a prayer unanswered when the answer isn't what we expected. Isn't no an answer? And when a "fatal" accident occurs, I feel like adding, "Isn't heaven an answer?"[1]

This glimpse into Amy's understanding of God challenges the soul. However, there are those—even among Christians—who have a much lower view of God's merciful hand.

William Barclay, an English theologian, wrote Bible commentaries that led many believers to love Christ more deeply—and at the same time sparked some controversy within the Christian community. When Barclay's twenty-one-year-old daughter and her fiancé were drowned in a yachting accident, Dr. Barclay was invited to talk about the accident on the BBC. He reminded the listeners that Jesus still performs miracles. Christ, he explained, had calmed the turmoil in his heart and his wife's so that they came through that terrible time still standing up.

In response to the broadcast, one person wrote an anonymous letter to Dr. Barclay: "I know why God killed your daughter. It was to save her from being corrupted by your heresies."

Of that message, Barclay wrote: "If I had had that writer's address I would have written back, not in anger—the inevitable blaze of anger was over in a flash—but in pity and I would have said to him, as John Wesley said to someone, 'Your God is my devil.' The day my daughter was lost at sea there was sorrow in the heart of God."[2] → *Did He mourn for me? For my baby? I shouldn't ask that...*

Time to Reflect

As you look at the heart of God today, do you see him to be more like Dr. Barclay—or the hostile letter writer? Ask God to show you his heart of love for you and those you love—and for those you find it difficult to love. *I know that He ♡s me. I know that He will/has comforted me... I'm just struggling to lean on Him → My head & my ♡ are at war.*

Prayer for the Day

Forgive me, Lord, when I assume I know what is best. I desire to know your heart. <u>Thank you for being patient with me when I judge your ways wrongfully, simply because I don't understand them,</u> I submit to your lordship and rest in your loving arms today. ↓

THIS → Father, help me work past this attitude. Help me to rest in you & your providence — your sovereignty. Knowing that it wasn't your will — your desire for me to lose my child. Remind me daily of your ♡ — that I can rest in you. Hold me on days when my sorrow tries to consume me. Father, I still pray for a miracle. But know, I will praise you — either way...

๛

Her View of God Changed Everything

> But as for me, my feet had almost slipped; I had nearly lost
> my foothold. For I envied the arrogant when I saw the
> prosperity of the wicked. They have no struggles; their
> bodies are healthy and strong. They are free from the bur-
> dens common to man; they are not plagued by human
> ills.... Surely in vain have I kept my heart pure.
>
> PSALM 73:2-5, 13

All of us at some time in our lives have breathed words similar to these. The psalmist begins this psalm with his ultimate conclusion, "Surely God is good to Israel, to those who are pure in heart" (v. 1). Yet, as he assessed his experience in the real world as of late, the psalmist had to confess that he felt let down. His feet were on the verge of slipping. What's the use of being good if you can be wicked and still seem to have such a carefree life? *This thought comes to mind for me... Why?*

But then this ancient journaler went on to record: "Till I entered the sanctuary of God" (v. 17). There everything became refocused as he stood in silence before God. It was there he understood the wicked's final destiny of ruin and wrote: *perspective*

> When I saw this, what turmoil filled my heart! I saw myself
> so stupid and so ignorant; I must seem like an animal to you,
> O God. But even so, you love me! You are holding my right
> hand! You will keep on guiding me all my life with your wis-

dom and counsel; and afterwards receive me into the glories of heaven! Whom have I in heaven but you? And I desire no one on earth as much as you! My health fails; my spirits droop, yet God remains! He is the strength of my heart; he is mine forever! He is Constant.

PSALM 73:21-26, LB

Truth prevails *if* we take the time and have the will to bring ourselves in line with it. In this case, the psalmist went from believing that God had nothing to offer him to discovering that God is enough in every circumstance.

It's been over thirty years since Joni Eareckson Tada was paralyzed by a diving accident. In the beginning, she begged God for healing. How could she live the rest of her life like this? Sometimes during that season she looked at others who had all their faculties and wondered what God was doing.

But today she tells us that she long ago abandoned those prayers of desperation. Instead, she says:

Jesus *didn't* pass me by. He *didn't* overlook me. He answered my prayer—He said "No." And I'm glad. A "no" answer has purged sin from my life, strengthened my commitment to Christ, and forced me to depend on grace. It has bound me with other believers, produced discernment, disciplined my mind, and taught me to spend my time wisely. It has stretched my hope, increased my faith, and strengthened my character. Being in this wheelchair has meant knowing Christ better. Feeling His strength every day.... Sometimes "no" is a better answer. Sometimes healing happens on the inside.[3] Good stuff.

Time to Reflect

Joni's view of God has made all the difference. She knows the character of God inside and out, and has had to depend on him for each moment. <u>Is your view of God big enough that you can accept the nos in life, and see each no as a yes to something better?</u> TH 16 – Rm. 8:28

Prayer for the Day

O Lord, I have such a long way to go in this area of my life with you. Thank you for the reminder that it takes years to make people deep enough that they can respond to you in this way. I want to go there, but I'll admit, I'm not eager to go the way Joni has had to go. Continue to shape my view of your character too, Father, so that it makes all the difference in my life.

Three

Will the Real Me Please Stand Up?

Surely you desire truth in the inner parts; you teach me wisdom in the inmost place.

PSALM 51:6

After being rejected a few times for being less than perfect, it became difficult for me to remain open and vulnerable and to admit when I was wrong. I reasoned that it was best to keep people at arm's length and to try to be as perfect as possible. However, as I've grown older, I've seen how vital it is to admit my own shortcomings, and to let others know that, like them, I am only a fellow struggler who is nothing without the power of Christ in me. THIS

One instance immediately comes to mind. I was speaking in Canada at a conference. My hostess was the dean of women at a seminary, an older woman who had traveled through much pain in life and permitted it to press into her a remarkably Christlike spirit. I had studied her throughout my visit and had learned much from her about how to respond under tension and stress.

My journal reveals how, at the end of the first day, I was annoyed because the meeting at which I'd been asked to speak that evening had gone on far too long. The next day was to be a demanding one, and no one seemed to be ready to get me back to my room where I could get a much-needed rest. The next morning, after sensing God's presence and strengthening as I spoke, I wrote:

> I fought being on edge last night. But A____ [my hostess] was total patience. A silent rebuke to me. No word was spoken; she simply manifested the Spirit of Christ. While I didn't verbalize any irritation, the body language was there, and the Father and I knew. How could I possibly speak to others until I repented of such immaturity? God, in kindness, moved today, perhaps in part because he had Gail in a good place: broken, needing his forgiveness and filling.

Whenever we go through moments or seasons of breaking, it's important to hold two things in tension: to honestly look within, taking responsibility for our thoughts and actions, and to eagerly look upward to Christ, who bids us come just as we are.

my attitude during the storm.

Time to Reflect

Would those who know you well say you are quick to face your own shortcomings? Has reading this brought back memories that you need to offer up to your Father in heaven? Picture him receiving you as you are.

Prayer for the Day

you would not refuse — that is where you start

Lord, you said you love a broken and contrite spirit. I come to you eager to rid myself of the weights that hang on me from the daily inner irritations in my life. Give me courage to admit my weaknesses to you and myself. Thank you for receiving me exactly as I am and for your infinite love.

If you need a broken life — use mine...

Four

֍

Jesus Shows Us the Father's Patience

And he [Jesus] sent messengers on ahead, who went into a Samaritan village to get things ready for him; but the people there did not welcome him, because he was heading for Jerusalem. When the disciples James and John saw this, they asked, "Lord, do you want us to call fire down from heaven to destroy them?" But Jesus turned and rebuked them, and they went to another village.

LUKE 9:52-56

All about Grace ↓

Jesus was sensitive to the realities of human failure. In the Gospels, time and again Jesus engaged those he met with a message of grace, urging them toward repentance and restoration, a new and better way. *Our example...*

It's easy for us to hold grudges toward those who have refused us a kindness or to expect the same behavior from them the next time. Not Jesus. Instead, he seems to lift the crown four inches over their heads, saying, "Try again, grow up into this crown—the next time you may get it right."

Jesus' generous spirit can be observed even during the moments of his anguish. He sadly watched his disciples sleep through three occasions when he had asked them to pray with him in the garden. When the ordeal was over, he did not say to them, "I'm through with you, let's get the B team!" No, he simply said, "Arise, let's go [to the next experience]."

When others disappoint us, we can learn much about what

27

which do I choose?

$a \rightarrow peace$
$b \rightarrow bitterness$

Our reactions should be from how Jesus responded in these situations. We have a choice to embrace the mind of Christ, or become arbitrary, opinionated, rigid judges.

Christ calls us to pray for the errant and hurting friend, to ask that through the pain of consequence, he or she will choose to do things differently the next time. The mind of Christ causes us to grieve greatly out of love and leads us to shower with restorative grace the one who has disappointed us.

It is a striking fact that Jesus never said a judgmental word to a repentant person. He knew the frailties of human nature and extended grace rather than anger toward those who recognized their failure. "Here's my hand," he simply said. "Let's start over." *— and over, and over, and over . . .*

Time to Reflect

In the Epistle of James we read, "Mercy triumphs over judgment!" (Jas 2:13). Think of a time someone extended mercy to you when you deserved judgment. Or remember a time when you were patient with someone who didn't deserve it. Consider the outcome of each had there been an absence of mercy. Give thanks that we have a Savior who gives us not what we deserve but what we need.

Prayer for the Day

Father, thank you for showing me your patience through your Son. I confess that I often feel superior when someone fails to do things right, but I want to be more like Jesus. Help me to let go of this tendency and embrace your ways throughout this day.

Five

My Friend, the Embezzler

Now one of the Pharisees invited Jesus to have dinner with him, so he went to the Pharisee's house and reclined at the table. When a woman who had lived a sinful life in that town learned that Jesus was eating at the Pharisee's house, she brought an alabaster jar of perfume, and as she stood behind him at his feet weeping, she began to wet his feet with her tears. Then she wiped them with her hair, kissed them and poured perfume on them....

Jesus said to her, "Your sins are forgiven."

The other guests began to say among themselves, "Who is this who even forgives sins?"

Jesus said to the woman, "Your faith has saved you; go in peace."

LUKE 7:36-38, 48-50

Whenever community is based on human goodness, a subtle fear spreads. Knowing how far we fall short of the standard that has been defined as goodness, we become increasingly anxious about owning up to the evil in our hearts. The prospect of being rejected by a group we love and admire makes it difficult to be transparent about our own fears and failures.

Gordon and I had been married only a few years when a friend whom we loved was caught embezzling money. More than twenty years later, I still look back on my reaction to this friend and her sin with much sadness. Instead of helping my

esp. when you've waited this long to tell it in a similar setting

friend face the facts of her wrongdoing, discover the causes of it deep within herself, and make things right, I became preoccupied with my own disappointment. I spent valuable time licking my own wounds.

The woman in this Scripture passage found in Jesus a "safe place" that revealed the compassionate heart of God for his wayward children. If we are to be Jesus to those who are struggling, we, too, must *be* a "safe place" for them. ThinkDIVAS.

I have often wondered if my colleague had tried to signal that she was in trouble. It is possible that, fearing my rejection, she could not bring herself to share the full truth until it was too late. But can a friendship be genuine if it harbors such a fear of rejection?

I could not have justified the sin of embezzlement, of course. Neither did Jesus treat the sinful actions of anyone glibly. At the same time, he did not "throw away" any person who was genuinely contrite in the wake of sin. His perspective was always built on the long-range view: "I'm not surprised by what has happened, and I grieve over the consequences you'll face. But I see your broken and sorrowful spirit, and I anticipate great things from you when you've learned from these wrong choices."

I wonder where my colleague would be today if I'd been someone with whom she felt she could be transparent. Had she confided in me her actions, I wish I could be sure that my response would have been deep concern rather than avoidance, a loving call to accountability and repentance rather than rejection. For whatever reason, she did not open her heart to me about the temptations or, later, her destructive actions. Her life might have been different today if she had felt free to take that first step. It was a hard lesson ... for both of us.

Father, I pray that you will lead me to someone I can be totally transparent to — a mentor — even @ 42 —

Are you a "safe haven" for people in trauma over choices that have led them far from the heart of God? Or do they tend to avoid you when they've "missed the mark"? Pray for humility to see your own weaknesses. When it comes to your own shortcomings, is there someone in your life to whom you are accountable? Are you being transparent with that person?

Prayer for the Day

"Lord, make me an instrument of your peace. Where there is hatred let me show love; where there is injury, pardon; where there is doubt, faith. O Master, grant that I might seek not so much to be consoled as to console; not so much to be understood as to understand; not so much to be loved as to love. For it is in giving that we receive; it is in pardoning that we are pardoned; it is in dying that we are born to eternal life" (Francis of Assisi).

Amen & Amen.

Six

The God Who Loves Enough to Pursue Us

> Two men went up to the temple to pray, one a Pharisee
> and the other a tax collector. The Pharisee stood up and
> prayed about himself: "God, I thank you that I am not like
> other men."
>
> LUKE 18:10-11

It's doubtful that any of us can become a safe haven for a person who has failed until we see our own need for forgiveness. Self-righteousness needs to be dealt a deathblow by the God who pursues us. François Fénelon, the notable French mystic, was right when he said,

> The most eminent graces turn to deadly poison if we rest on
> them in self-complacent security. This was the sin of the
> fallen angels; as soon as they looked on their *exalted state* as
> their own assured possession, they became enemies of God
> and were driven forth from the Kingdom.[4]

One day a friend asked me if I had a case of "good flesh." He didn't mean it as a put-down; he knew I had tried hard to live as honorably as I could. But what he was asking me was, had I grown even slightly self-righteous? Was I harboring thoughts so deep within me that I was hardly aware of them, that God was fortunate to have me on his team? Oh, yes, I knew it was only by God's grace that I was able to do anything right. But I

32

suspected that a subtle, nagging, and very ugly spiritual pride had also grown alongside the good deeds and the calm spirit. Was this the *exalted state* of which Fénelon spoke?

All of this came to a head for me one terrible night in my forty-ninth year. It's hard for me to recall what triggered it, but an accumulation of negative feelings suddenly reached explosive potential within me. I found myself ready to lash out at whomever or whatever stood in my path. If it had not been so late at night with everyone asleep, perhaps I would have vented things that would have hurt those I love. As it was, I had no one to face but God and self as I fought one of the most violent spiritual battles I have ever faced.

In those unforgettable, lonely hours, I was forced to take a hard look at myself; image and pretense were stripped away. This was not a time to study anyone else; it was rather a time to look exclusively at Gail, with her deep need for forgiveness for an ugly spiritual pride. Jesus saved his hottest anger and his harshest words for the religiously proud. Was I one of them? If so, I was going to renounce this "good flesh" and make a fresh pilgrimage to the cross along with the most repentant of visible sinners.

The Pharisee's prayer was a "good flesh" prayer. The other man, who because of his profession was considered by good people to be among the worst of the worst, simply prayed: "God, have mercy on me, a sinner" (v. 13). For this spirit, he received the Lord's commendation.

Most of us have difficulty remembering the last time we prayed like that. Thankfully, we have a pursuing, kind God. He gives us grace to look at ourselves honestly and then forgives in response to our heart cry of repentance. I remember coming to the end of the anguish of those hours and feeling free—washed, humbled, more clear-sighted about my real self than I'd been for a long time. There have been, and will continue to be, subsequent washings, for "self-righteousness" is *not* a malady from which one is cured instantly. Rather, it requires a simple day-by-day mastering.

Time to Reflect

Thomas à Kempis said, "It would not hurt you at all to consider yourself less righteous than others, but it will be disastrous for you to consider yourself better than even one person." What does this say to us about the value of humility? When was the last time God pursued you in order to extend his forgiveness to you? What does this say to you about the character of God?

Prayer for the Day

Lord, I don't want to be indifferent to your pursuit of me. I repent of thinking I am better than other people ... even one other person. Do a freeing work in my soul today, Father, as I deal with my self-righteous attitudes. Thank you that your everlasting arms are there for me.

Not just as an overall BUT even one...
do I see that in myself —
→ I often forget sin is sin → there
aren't varying
degrees.
→ My job - to ♥ people -
ALL people where they
are & remember I am the
least of these!!

Seven

The God Who Precedes Us

For the Lord will go before you, the God of Israel will be
your rear guard.

ISAIAH 52:12

(handwritten margin notes: "How on time!", "merciful", "committed suicide", "weak", "before reading this")

What a shock! Even though it happened many years ago,
the day my sister-in-law took her own life is indelibly
etched on my soul. She left ten children, the offspring of a
blended family. When the call came, I was at a mother-and-
daughter dinner with our young daughter, Kristy. Because I had
been studying about how Jesus reacted to the news of his good
friend Lazarus' death, that was the first thought that came to
my mind. Jesus didn't panic in the face of death.

Asking our Father to give me his Son's mind in the coming
days made all the difference. There was an inner calm that I
knew was a direct result of being prepared ahead of time by
what I had meditated on earlier. Over the years this has happened many times to us. We know because our journals attest
to it. They are an invaluable tool in recalling God's inner
promptings to develop in certain areas of our characters; without a written record this important preparation of heart is forgotten. However, if we listen to his inner guidance and obey it,
we have the assurance of his sustaining grace. God does not
want us to fall into situations for which we are unprepared.

In the hours before and after the Crucifixion, Jesus did things on behalf of the disciples that they could not have appreciated at the time. He prepared the way for them by going *before* them at important moments in their lives together. He saw to it that the Upper Room was arranged in order that they might enjoy strength-giving camaraderie.

After Jesus' crucifixion, the women at the tomb were told to "tell his disciples and Peter, 'He is going *ahead of you* into Galilee'" (Mk 16:7, emphasis mine). Tell his disciples *and Peter.* Because Peter had denied his Lord, Jesus knew that Peter would need comfort more than anyone.

Later, after another night of defeat, the Lord was kind enough to prepare a breakfast for a group of tired and chilly fisherman/disciples *before* they reached the shore (see Jn 21:9-12). Finally, he has gone *before* us all to prepare a home in heaven.

God continues to go before us today, preparing the way for us even in our darkest moments. One morning when I was fighting the temptation to fear the day ahead, I was amazed and strengthened by my early morning quiet before the Lord. This is what I read out of Oswald Chambers' *My Utmost for His Highest:*

> God says, "Never will I leave you: never will I forsake you." So that we can say with confidence, "The Lord is my helper; I will not be afraid. What can man do to me?" (See Hebrews 13:5-6.) ... This does not mean that I will not be tempted to fear, but I will remember God's say-so. I will be full of courage, like a child "bucking himself up" to reach the standard his father wants.... When there is nothing and no one to help you, say—"But, the Lord is my Helper, this second, in my present outlook...." It doesn't matter what evil or wrong may be in the way, He has said—"I will never leave you."[5]

The sense of God's care in the reading is something I will always recall with gratitude. I felt myself relaxed in God's everlasting arms in a way that kept me from becoming overwhelmed by the circumstances surrounding me. I knew this was God's doing— and it was marvelous in my eyes.

Time to Reflect

Is it possible that we have been in too great a hurry to reflect upon the things God has been preparing for us? Write down a few times when you also have seen his preparatory hand.

Dad — being sick
being called m... *[handwritten]*

Dave — ministry ups & downs *[handwritten]*

Prayer for the Day

It both excites me and brings a measure of dread to think that you might be preparing me for something difficult right now, Lord. But, no matter what, I want to instinctively walk in your ways. You said to ask you boldly for your help—and so I come boldly to you now to ask for the heart to remember these things day to day to day.

[handwritten]
Help me to remember, that when this is done & I am left alone w/ my thoughts & the quiet to know I am not alone. Most will forget this baby... save you & me. Help me to see the marvelous in this. Reveal to me that which you are teaching. I'm still trying to understand.

Eight

The God Who Carries Us

I have upheld you since you were conceived, and have carried you since your birth. Even to your old age and gray hairs I am he, I am he who will sustain you. I have made you and I will carry you.

mem.

God carries us. He is the Shepherd who picks up his lost sheep and gently carries him out of the wilderness back to the sheepfold.

When we fall, it is carrying grace that sustains us. And it is this carrying grace that should be celebrated, *not the one being carried*. Without it, we who fail would remain immobilized where we stumbled. Without it, we would eventually turn back and quit. But this carrying grace of God lifts us to our feet and helps us take our first tentative steps forward again. This is possible because of his everlasting arms.

getting up is poss

One day I sat at an airport gate waiting for a flight. A small child ran back and forth among the passengers. Suddenly he tripped and fell, his forehead taking the brunt of the blow. When he looked up, his eyes already wet with tears, he sought his mother's face. She came toward him, and his arms reached out, seeking her closeness. She picked him up and let him sob out his pain and maybe his embarrassment on her shoulder.

Hers were the motions of carrying grace. As she toted him

Sam falling @ church today ↓

on her shoulder, he trusted in her ability to carry him safely, even though he was *unable to see where he was going, only where he had been.* He might not have called it carrying grace, but he surely accepted it. A beautiful picture, I think, of our relationship to our heavenly Father.

If we, like others who have known pain, are intact today with a heart's desire to serve; if Gordon and I walk together, our relationship welded more deeply than ever; if we have a sensitivity toward those who are falling in a hundred ways, it is not because of anything in us. We have simply received carrying grace. We take no credit for it. How can you boast about a gift?

In the mid-1800s, Henry Baker, an Anglican clergyman, obviously understood such Shepherd love. When asked to compile a new hymnal for his church, he wrote and added "The King of Love My Shepherd Is." The hymnal sold over sixty million copies. When Baker was dying, his last words came from the third stanza of his hymn:

reminds me of the song I am → *Oh gently lay your head upon my chest & I will comfort you like a mother — while you rest.*

> Perverse and foolish, oft I strayed,
> But yet in love He sought me,
> And on His shoulder gently laid,
> And home, rejoicing, brought me.[6]

Even in the reading of these words, the shoulders and body relax because we have a great God who cares enough to pick us up, insisting that together, he and we can make it.

Key — not on my own !

39

Time to Reflect

Consider a time when you needed "carrying grace" but instinctively tried to handle the situation on your own. How could that experience have been different, had you allowed your heavenly Shepherd to minister carrying grace to you?

Prayer for the Day

Father, today I want to avail myself of your shepherding love. Not only the staff that draws me near, but also the rod of rebuke that reminds me that I must be disciplined when I stray from your carrying grace. Teach me more of your Shepherd's heart.

Nine

The God Who Was Mistreated

To this you were called, because Christ suffered for you, leaving you an example, that you should follow in his steps.... When they hurled their insults at him, he did not retaliate; when he suffered, he made no threats. Instead, he entrusted himself to him who judges justly.

1 PETER 2:21, 23-24;
SEE ALSO MATTHEW 27:27-32

must follow X's example

No principle has meant more to Gordon and me—or challenged us more—than this one. When our lives evidence the fruit of repentance, yet we continue to experience the judgment and misunderstanding of others, we instinctively want to defend and protect ourselves. However, at these times Christ's response must become an active part, hour by hour, of our heart attitude.

tit + tat ≠ good

Like any leader, Amy Carmichael knew what it was like to be misunderstood by others. Once when a letter arrived that was greatly upsetting to her, she heard the Lord whisper six words to her over and over, "Let it be; think of Me." She wanted

To share her "crumb of comfort at once, and tell them not to weigh flying words, or let their peace be in the mouths of men.... If He remembers, what does it matter that others forget?" *That's good...*

Thus being comforted and filled with inner sweetness, we

[handwritten at top: Choose to not fight back — don't add fuel to the fire.]

can thank Him for all who trample unawares upon us, talking smooth nothings. For we know, just because they can do it so unconsciously, so easily, and with so airy a grace, that they, at least, were never laid in iron; and is *that* not good to know?[7]

Another one of my favorite people in church history is Catherine Booth. Her husband, William, the founder of the Salvation Army, was often slandered and criticized. But when the raw and biting comments of religious leaders were directed at Catherine, William found that more difficult to accept than anything that had ever happened to him. His challenge to Catherine in that moment is powerful.

I cannot understand how they can possibly treat you and the work of God thus. If it had been me, I should have scarcely marveled, but you, it is absolutely confounding.... I am sure I hardly know what to advise. That which comes first is give them up and do it with a high hand. Then second thoughts say that ten years hence the treatment we personally receive from these "leaders" (in religion) will be as NOTHING.

We shall all but have forgotten it. But our treatment of the work of God, our forbearance and humility and meekness and perseverance under and in the face of difficulties will be everything.[8]

[handwritten left margin: I must think long term not the hurt now.]

Their choice not to fight back is at least part of the reason the Salvation Army has continued to be a light to suffering and rejected humanity for over one hundred years. To have made lesser choices and pursued vindication would have brought momentary relief to the Booths, but not long-term growth and inner well-being.

The Booths' example has continued to inspire succeeding generations of Army people; over the years it has also been a standard Gordon and I have set for ourselves, a straightedge against which we measure our response to slander, accusations, and lies. Easy? Not humanly speaking, but it is during such difficult times, when we allow it, that God works in us to make his heart our own.

Time to Reflect

Augustine once said, "Deliver me from the lust of always vindicating myself." Has this "lust" gained access to your soul? Pray over some specific situations where you need to exercise Christ's response.

Prayer for the Day

Lord, I admit that there have been times I have been tempted to respond in socially acceptable but spiritually empty ways: hate, litigation, condemnation. Help me to renounce these choices, and to relinquish the *need to be right.* Thank you for being the God who shows us the way, and who daily gives us the strength to walk in it.

this is what we were talking about tonight — Condemnation of lifestyles that challenged my beliefs —

this one may be tough — one that I will learn quickly!

The God Who Owns It All

John replied, "A man can receive only what is given him from heaven. You yourselves can testify that I said, 'I am not the Christ but am sent ahead of him.' The bride belongs to the bridegroom. The friend who attends the bridegroom waits and listens for him, and is full of joy when he hears the bridegroom's voice. That joy is mine, and it is now complete. He must become greater; I must become less."

JOHN 3:27-30

When Gordon and I were at the lowest point in our marriage, years ago, I found myself recalling a sermon my husband had preached many times. He taught us that John the Baptist was sought after and popular with the multitudes. But when the day came for him to introduce the crowds to Jesus, though it meant he would lose both the crowds and his job, John never lost his God.

John's attitude and actions were exactly what Gordon and I needed to learn during those months of heartbreak. *First*, we saw that John considered himself a steward of everything, not the owner (v. 27). So when Jesus took the crowds, it was fine, for John knew all along that they never belonged to him.

Second, John knew who he *was* and who he was *not*. He had reminded them all along that he was not the Christ, even

* John the "best man" to the bridegroom.

though they tried to suggest he might be (v. 28). His identity was based on the truth, not ego gratification. ʰˣ⁾

Third, John knew the role or mission he was to play—the best man, not the bridegroom (v. 29). The bridegroom had come; the best man's job was simply to point out the groom, and to be sure that everyone's attention was riveted on him alone. John had one objective in his life: Jesus must become greater; John must become less (v. 30).

Did losing the crowds not matter to John? Of course it mattered. He was human. But God gave John the strength to face these changes as they came. John was not leaning on John. John's understanding of who God is and of what he had been called to do saved John from cynicism and anger.

As we serve the Lord, it is important that we have an accurate understanding of who God is and what he is calling us to do. So much heartbreak can be avoided if we know and embrace the truth about God's character. Then we can trust his heart, relinquish our *right to ourselves,* and even flourish through seemingly difficult circumstances.

These truths kept Gordon and me as we sought after a true view of the heart of God. We knew, at the core of our beings, that we could save our lives only by losing them. This kind of living is possible because God fills people with his Spirit. Whenever we begin to drift into "pity-pot" territory, we come back to this defining moment for John and give thanks. Thomas à Kempis put it this way: "Whenever a man inordinately desires anything, he instantly loses inward peace. The proud and covetous are never at rest, while the poor and lowly in spirit pass their life in continual peace."⁹

Time to Reflect *where is my identity?*

Are you an owner or a steward? Is your identity too closely linked to your job or work? What would happen to your faith if the rug were pulled out from under you, if you lost it all? Could you say with Christian in John Bunyan's *Pilgrim's Progress,* "I am on the bottom and it is firm"?

"He must increase, but I must decrease" (v. 30, KJV). In what ways do you see that verse operating in your own life?

Prayer for the Day

Thank you, Lord, for John the Baptist. His life teaches me so much about how to respond to change, to breaking, and to your sovereign choices in my life. With the psalmist I say, "My eyes are fixed on you, O Sovereign Lord.... When my spirit grows faint within me it is you who know my way" (Ps 141:8; 142:3).

Finish the race - start to finish must start running - not sitting + waiting I DO IT NOW...

Section Two

෧෭

Making Pain Your Ally

Life can be tough. Pain and challenge touch each of us, but we cope with them in different ways. In the midst of crisis, we often go through stages of response, each with its own temptations—the temptation to self-pity, for example. I know now how significant my own response to these inner movements and enticements became in my effort to progress beyond suffering.

When it became my turn for pain, I knew I had to obey God in spite of how I felt. I chose to talk myself through certain emotions. I owned the truth and acted on it, no matter what. I forced myself to look honestly at my heart rather than run from the discomfort and blame others. You will see in this section how the choice to make pain your ally can make all the difference.

Eleven

Beautiful Caves of Pain

I will give you the treasures of darkness, riches stored in
secret places, so that you may know that I am the Lord,
the God of Israel, who summons you by name.

ISAIAH 45:3

Once I read about scuba divers who explore undersea caves
and find magnificent beauty in sea life and natural forma-
tions. You couldn't get me that far down into the water—much
less into an undersea cave. In the same way, few people would
ever consider taking on pain voluntarily.

But just as the scuba diver finds treasures in the darkness of
the deep, so there are strange and wonderful treasures found in
the darkness of life's pain—the "secret places," as the prophet
Isaiah writes. In the days of my life when I felt darkness engulf
me, I became acutely aware that each minute I had a choice to
make: To seek treasures or to succumb to sadness.

A dear friend sent me a "treasure" that often reminded me of
the presence and nearness of God. It was a simple card with an
inscription taken from a cellar in Cologne, Germany, where
Jews had been hidden during the Holocaust. It read:

I believe in love even when I don't feel it.
I believe in God even when he is silent.

For months I carried that affirmation in my purse, pulling it out when I needed a word of hope. It was a gentle reminder not only to pull myself together but to intercede for those who are unable to see anything but their present gloom. The treasure was in knowing that if God could bring Jews through the Holocaust, he can handle my small challenges.

When we are in pain it's easy to clench our fists and come out fighting. But no one ever receives the great messages hidden in pain with fisted hands. If we open our hands when the disconcerting experiences come, our darkness will reveal many treasures—and draw us closer to our Father's heart. In the words of Amy Carmichael:

> Hast thou no scar?...
> As the Master shall the Servant be,
> And pierced are the feet that follow Me;
> But thine are whole, can he have followed far
> Who has no wound? No scar?[1]

Time to Reflect

When you and I go into caves of darkness, do we clench our fists or reach out toward the treasure and the light? What has the Lord taught us in these beautiful caves? List a few things he's taught you and give thanks.

Prayer for the Day

Lord, if you have something to teach me in these present difficult circumstances, I trust you to show me clearly—in your time. Help me to follow you even though I cannot see very far ahead of me right now.

Twelve
❧

The Temptation to Turn Back

> We do not want you to be uninformed, brothers, about
> the hardships we suffered in the province of Asia. We were
> under great pressure, far beyond our ability to endure, so
> that we despaired even of life. Indeed, in our hearts we felt
> the sentence of death. But this happened that we might
> not rely on ourselves but on God.
>
> 2 CORINTHIANS 1:8-9

The apostle Paul certainly must have understood the temptation to turn back. He had been stoned in Lystra, beaten in Philippi, bothered in Berea, and barely tolerated in Athens. Prolonged stress from persistent hostility must have brought fatigue, weakness, and discouragement.

As I read Luke's account of Paul's fifty-mile journey from Athens to Corinth, it is easy to read between the lines and see all these things dominating his spirit. He must have been weary as he entered the city, and more than a little discouraged as he looked up and saw the temple of Aphrodite, home of a thousand consecrated prostitutes, ruling the skyline. Before him in the marketplace loomed a cosmopolitan city rife with sensualism, materialism, and paganism. Sound familiar?

Where do you begin when you feel discredited, beaten, weary, and alone? Later, looking back at those earliest moments, Paul would write to the Corinthians about his first visit: "I came to you in weakness and fear, and with much trembling" (1 Cor

2:3).

It showed. Every indication is that Paul preached a defensive message in the early days of the Corinth mission. Gone for a short while were the old charisma and the offensive capacity to charge ahead and ignore opposition. Absent was the vigor that took on every opponent, caring little about what others thought.

When at first the Corinthian Jews resisted the gospel, Paul lapsed into anger and told them their blood would never be on his hands. He'd done his best, he said, and now he would turn to the Gentiles. Paul was a man succumbing to the effects of long-endured stress. There even may have been a temptation to indulge in a bit of self-pity. Luke the physician apparently thought it was important to let the reader know that even the great apostle had days when his perspective flagged.

Time to Reflect

Perhaps you have been tempted to turn back. It happens to us all sooner or later. Do you find encouragement in the fact that God brought the apostle Paul through untold agony—and in the same way, he will bring you and I through too? Think on these things today.

Prayer for the Day

Lord, sometimes I don't even have enough energy or the facility to concentrate enough to pray. Turning back seems the only option. I hope others are praying for me right now. And I'm comforted to recall your promise to pray for us (see Heb 7:23-25).

Thirteen

❧

Suffering Love

> You need to know that I carry with me at all times a huge
> sorrow. It's an enormous pain deep within me, and I'm
> never free of it. I'm not exaggerating—Christ and the
> Holy Spirit are my witnesses. It's the Israelites … if there
> were a way I could be cursed by the Messiah so they could
> be blessed by him, I'd do it in a minute.
>
> ROMANS 9:1-3, THE MESSAGE

I watch Paul moving from city to city on his own journey, and I marvel at his intensity. Because he loved Christ and his Jewish brothers and sisters deeply, he was motivated to bring them together. Such determination could only bring heartbreak on certain occasions when his dream was not realized. Earnest loving always brings pain.

This is the risk each of us takes when we care deeply. The more we love, the greater the pain when something does not go according to plan. Nicholas Wolterstorff addressed this as he worked through the loss of his twenty-five-year-old son, who perished in a mountain-climbing accident. Nicholas realized that much of his pain grew out of the intensity of his love for his son.

> Love in our world is suffering love. Some do not suffer much, though, for they do not love much. Suffering is for loving. If I hadn't loved him, there wouldn't be this agony.

This, said Jesus, is the command of the Holy One: "You shall love your neighbor as yourself." In commanding us to love, God invites us to suffer. God is love. That is why he suffers. To love our suffering, sinful world is to suffer. God so suffered for the world that he gave up his only Son to suffering. The one who does not see God's suffering does not see his love. God is suffering love.[2]

I would not trade the absence of pain for a shallow love. To love with intensity today seems rare because such devotion takes an enormous investment of time, energy, and self-giving. But those who have so loved, saying yes to pain, will tell us that it has been worth it all. Oh, it may not seem so when going through the intense moments of anguish, as Wolterstorff describes so well. But when one looks at the long view of life—perspective regained—a sweetness in our walk with God is ours, a closeness that is hard to explain to those who look on.

George Matheson, the great preacher-hymn writer, went completely blind when he was eighteen years old. He wrote of the *love that would not let him go* on an evening in June 1882 on the day of his sister's marriage: "Something happened to me, which was known only to myself, and which caused me the most severe mental suffering. The hymn was the fruit of that suffering."[3]

Most think he was remembering a deep love he once had for a woman who broke off their engagement when she learned he was going blind. The fruit of that suffering love has been felt for two hundred years by millions of us as we reflect on his hymn.

Time to Reflect

Perhaps as you have read this you have been aware that loving deeply has brought about suffering in your own life. Where has deep loving taken you? If possible, write a few sentences about it and read them to yourself to help you see where you have been and how you have grown. Give thanks for God's continued love for you.

Prayer for the Day

"O love that will not let me go. I rest my weary soul in Thee; I give Thee back the life I owe, that in Thine ocean depths its flow may richer, fuller be. O Joy that seekest me through pain, I cannot close my heart to Thee; I trace the rainbow through the rain, and feel the promise is not vain that morn shall tearless be."[4] Jesus, help me to surrender to your suffering love this day.

Fourteen

໒ৎ

Teachable or Resistant?

Find rest, O my soul, in God alone; my hope comes from
him. He alone is my rock and my salvation; he is my
fortress, I will not be shaken.

PSALM 62:5-6

When pain or discontinuity in life comes, it's easy to shut
down on God and believe the worst rather than learning
from our present circumstances. We will not be able to make
pain our ally until we remain open to God in the midst of it.

We can receive only when our hands are open and empty. I'm
not advocating that we invite pain in some masochistic way. But
when the disconcerting experiences come, instead of crying,
"It's not fair," we can say, "Teach me, Lord." If we resist God's
comfort at such times, we have to endure not only the agony of
the situation but the loss of the awareness of God's tender companionship and present grace.

Michael Quoist once wrote:

As long as a child plays quietly, his mother remains in the
kitchen preparing dinner. But if he does something naughty
and hurts himself, his screams will bring the mother running
to help him. Despite his behavior, she is there, more attentive
and loving than ever.

The child ... can rebel against his hurt. He can throw himself on the floor; he can kick the piece of furniture on which he hurt himself; he can strike out at his mother who is trying to help him. But then he suffers even more, for his pain remains and now he has to be in it alone—alone with his frustration.

If he loves his mother, he goes beyond his pain and throws himself into her arms. She does not take the hurt away, but in holding her child, she bears the hurt with him. [5]

In precisely the same way, we can choose in our pain an attitude that further separates us from the Father or that draws us closer to him. It all depends on the outer posture of our hands and the inner posture of our hearts.

Time to Reflect

Think of the last time pain was your companion. Did you open your hands, or clench them? François Fénelon once said, "Open your heart; we heal our wounds by not hugging them." Think of a time when because you were open and teachable, God's presence was real and intimate. Can you hear yourself saying to people, "I wouldn't want to go through that again, but I can think of only a few times in my Christian life when my trust and faith grew as much"?

Prayer for the Day

Father, help me to learn the ways of your Son, who brought all things to you with an open, willing heart. I renounce the idea that I am entitled to a pain-free life. Help me not to resist the "fellowship of your sufferings."

Fifteen
᪥

Allowing Others "In"

Then Jesus went with his disciples to a place called
Gethsemane, and he said to them, "Sit here while I go
over there and pray." He took Peter and the two sons of
Zebedee along with him, and he began to be sorrowful
and troubled. Then he said to them, "My soul is overwhelmed with sorrow to the point of death. Stay here and
keep watch with me."

MATTHEW 26:36-38

I'm a New Englander. We are known for our rugged indi-
vidualism and for our resourcefulness. For years I fed this
notion in my own life. The women I trained got the message
that I could manage the tough experiences alone. Then pain
came. And because I had not been transparent about my weaknesses before, my friends didn't know what to do with me. This
was my fault, not theirs.

As a missionary-physician in Zaire, Dr. Helen Roseveare suffered terribly during the rebellions of the early sixties. At first
she was verbally abused and harassed. Then one night the suffering took on a much more evil expression when she was
repeatedly raped and beaten by rebels.

It was fortunate that, prior to this ghastly season in her life,
Helen had learned how to let people "in." During a period of
ill health, she had to be cared for by those she had gone to serve.

This was difficult for Helen, who bemoaned the fact that her illness was taking her staff away from other patients. Her fierce streak of independence was tempered, however, when one of her "disciples" explained to her that the *only time they felt she needed them* was when she was ill. The gentle rebuke prompted a change in Helen that lasted long after the sickness and even the rape had assaulted her body.

Think of the supernatural power it took for Helen not only to forgive, but to return to the place and to the people who harmed her, there to continue her service in the name of Christ. Because she returned and forgave, a hospital was built, thousands were cared for, scores were trained in medicine, and the response to her personal witness became a hundred times more powerful. But it had its roots in seeing that she needed others.

We serve a Savior who was willing to lean on his friends at the most vulnerable time of his life, in the Garden of Gethsemane. The disciples were allowed to look on as their Lord was overwhelmed by sorrow. How is it, then, that we as his disciples refuse to show our weaknesses to each other—even though we say we want to follow in his steps?

Time to Reflect

Do you allow for your own vulnerable seasons without shame? Or do you pretend to be OK to others? When was the last time you let someone know you needed help?

Prayer for the Day

Lord, please forgive me if I appear too proud to seek help and thereby deny another the opportunity to minister to me. Thank you, Lord Jesus, for showing us the way in your darkest hour.

Getting Attention Through Calamity

Come to me, all you who are weary and burdened, and I
will give you rest. Take my yoke upon you and learn from
me, for I am gentle and humble in heart, and you will find
rest for your souls.

MATTHEW 11:28-29

When we endure pain, it can be an overwhelming temptation to look around to see if anyone is noticing. Will
someone come alongside to offer attention? If so, a second
temptation presents itself, the urge to unload everything that
is on our minds: our anger, our frustration, and our cries of
injustice.

A dark part of the human spirit claws for attention, no matter what it takes to get it. There are even those who choose pain
because it brings attention they would not otherwise receive.
Some have called it *drawing attention to self through calamity*.
But what we get from people may cause us to forfeit what we
could receive most intimately from God himself. Brigid
Hermann challenges us concerning these things:

Did we but know the things that belong to our peace in times
of sorrow and adversity, our instinct of spiritual self-preserva-
tion would urge us to hug silence. The vice of airing one's
soul to any and every person whom we believe likely to prove
sympathetic and helpful is eating the very core of reality out
of those who practice it. There are times in our spiritual life

when we need a human counselor and guide, but nowhere are wisdom and self-restraint more imperative than here. Our Protestant practice allows us to give free rein to our craving for sympathy, to pour out our confidences with as much profusion and intimacy of detail as we are inclined to ... keeping evil memories green.[6]

Ira White, a woman who lived in my hometown, is an encouraging example of how to balance the need for human assistance without living off of the sympathy of others. At sixty-one Ira was told she would soon be totally blind. She decided *not* to tell her husband, lest his sympathy ruin her resolve to triumph over this, the greatest test of her life.

Instead, she told her daughter-in-law, who played games with Ira which they called "handicaps." She blindfolded her mother-in-law and gave Ira easy tasks like dialing the phone, washing and drying dishes, vacuuming, and preparing meat and vegetables. By the time Mrs. White told the rest of her family and friends, she was doing so well that there was no need for her to become the center of attention.

Mrs. White was blind for two years, then miraculously she regained her eyesight for another twenty years. She went back to creative arts school and learned how to paint and write. At age eighty, when Ira lost her husband, she opened her garage as a studio for children to learn to paint. There were regular slumber parties and art exhibits. And when she once again lost her sight, at the age of eighty-seven, she decided she still could write a book—and she did. God sustained her, day by day by day.

"The arrow seen beforehand slacks its flight." The ancient martyrs, who were going to be thrown into the lions' den, would sometimes go alone to the arena the day before they were to be killed. There they looked up at the seats where Caesar and the other spectators would sit. They looked at the iron door where the enemy would enter. Then they imagined themselves being thrown to the lions. Having imagined the worst, they could then face certain death with courage. Because of this, their victory was won *before* the day of their agony.

Time to Reflect

Write down your thoughts about what you have read. How might you implement this reading in your daily life? Do you know an "Ira White" whom you should be seeking out so as to learn from him or her?

Prayer for the Day

Lord, show me how to let others help me without basking in an unhealthy need for attention. Give me the mind of Christ, whose love and need for you always took precedence over his need for others.

Seventeen

క్రు

Ultimate Goals of Pain

All praise to the God and Father of our Master, Jesus the
Messiah! Father of all mercy! God of all healing counsel!
He comes alongside us when we go through hard times,
and before you know it, he brings us alongside someone
else who is going through hard times so that we can be
there for that person just as God was there for us.

2 CORINTHIANS 1:3-4, THE MESSAGE

When we have friends in our home, we sometimes ask each
guest a series of questions as a kind of "icebreaker." The
final question is, "At what point in your life did you feel closest
to God?"

I've listened to hundreds of responses to that query in our
living rooms over the years. The majority of answers focus on a
moment when life seemed its darkest. It was a terrible time,
many say, but God touched their lives with a promise, a personal
insight, a sense of supernatural strength or courage. It's not
unusual for people to add that it was a never-to-be-forgotten
encounter and one for which they will always be deeply thankful. What does this say to us?

Our intimacy with the Lord reaches some of its highest
peaks when we are at points of greatest personal need. God
desires to bring ultimate good and growth out of those difficult moments. However, this is a principle one needs to
ponder *before* encountering significant pain.

Jesus did this as he prayed in the Garden—anticipating the pain, he said yes to it. "Now my soul is deeply troubled. Shall I pray, 'Father, save me from what lies ahead'? But that is the very reason why I came! Father, bring glory and honor to your name'" (Jn 12:27-28, LB).

Amy Carmichael observed that *only One who prayed that prayer for Himself could pray so for another.* If relief, ease, and simple answers are our aim, then the prayers we pray for others won't do much for them. "A fountain cannot reach higher than its spring."[7]

More than once I've watched a friend or acquaintance pass through a terrible moment in life—grief, betrayal, failure—and I've been impressed that such people frequently seem to possess a remarkable amount of serenity and determination in spite of the fact that we who stand by and watch expect a total meltdown. As bystanders, we imagine ourselves in the same situation and assume that we could not make it if we were in that situation. What we often do not factor in is that the Spirit of God provides a special grace during those especially difficult times that may not be provided or experienced or even visualized by onlookers.

Bystanders at the grisly execution of Stephen, the first Christian martyr, might have been horrified at the pain he was going through as he slowly died under the rain of stones thrown by his persecutors. But Stephen seems to have experienced remarkable grace. He even had the capacity to pray for his enemies. Both goals of pain were realized in Stephen: Others were comforted by his life, and God received praise.

Time to Reflect

Charles Spurgeon once wrote: "I bear my willing witness that I owe more to the fire, and the hammer, and the file, than to anything else in my Lord's workshop. I sometimes question whether I have ever learned anything except through the rod. When my schoolroom is darkened, I see most."[8] Can you attest to this today?

Prayer for the Day

Lord, help me to never waste my pain. I often feel weak, but I'm thankful for those you have sent to me who show me your carrying grace. Help me to accept responsibility for my responses to pain so that someday I can look back and see that I didn't act like a victim, but instead, I saw your purposes at work.

Eighteen

Looking for the Humor

A cheerful look brings joy to the heart.

PROVERBS 15:30

By nature, I tend to be a serious person, so I am drawn to those who find humor in everything. A friend of mine who sustained a long period of depression told me she learned the therapeutic value of laughter through her preschooler. The child had fallen on her back in a mud puddle. Instead of crying, as her mother expected, the little girl looked up at the trees from where she was lying and exclaimed, "Look at the pretty leaves, Mommy!" And my friend laughed.

One of my "book" friends, Samuel Logan Brengle, gave his life over fifty years ago to the poor as an evangelist and pastor. One night in Boston, Brengle was accosted by a drunken, angry man who threw a brick at Brengle, hitting him on the head. The old evangelist was seriously injured and for several weeks hung between life and death. Incapacitated for more than eighteen months, Brengle endured periodic bouts of depression and headaches for the rest of his life.

During his recuperation, Brengle wrote a short book that was distributed around the world by the Salvation Army. It was translated into a score of languages and became a remarkable resource to hundreds of thousands of people. When people tried to give him compliments for his book, he would simply respond, "Well, if there had been no little brick, there would have been no little book!"⁹

One friend who has taught me much about finding the humor in our misfortunes wrote a Christmas letter to her friends soon after she gave her life to Christ. Meg had experienced kidney failure the year before, and unless she had a transplant, she would need dialysis at least three times a week for the rest of her life. In her letter she wrote:

Last July, when my kidneys pooped out, death came very close and seemed very real. But after my head was cleared of toxins, after I "came back," every day became a bonus—extra time. It seems as though I traded in a set of kidneys (which would have given out eventually anyhow, along with the rest of my body) for a relationship with God (which won't).... I must admit that if I had been drawing up the plan for my life, I might have been a little easier on me. Maybe I would have opted for flat feet or itchy skin ... —something a little less dramatic—but "His thoughts are above our thoughts, and his ways above our ways."

Time to Reflect

Think about the people you enjoy having around you when you are going through a time of discontinuity. Do they increase your ability to see the humor in your situation, or are they apt to weaken you through too much negative talk? Are you also able to bring hope through humor in the lives of others?

Prayer for the Day

Dear Lord, I know how good it feels to laugh, and I don't laugh or find the humor in things nearly enough. Forgive me. Thank you for the people you have put in my life who can help me see the "colored leaves" when I'm in the mud.

Nineteen

Jesus Can Handle Our Doubts

Strengthen the feeble hands, steady the knees that give way; say to those with fearful hearts, "Be strong, do not fear; your God will come."

ISAIAH 35:3-4

Someone wisely said, "God doesn't always lighten our load, sometimes he strengthens our backs." Near the end of John the Baptist's ministry, while he was in prison, he went through a time of apparent weakness and questioning. He sent this message to Jesus, "Are you really the one we are waiting for, or shall we keep on looking?" (Mt 11:2, LB).

What was behind John's question? A kind of doubt. Perhaps Jesus was not acting in a way or at a speed that met John's expectations. But Jesus did not rebuke John. Rather, he sent back what must have been a most courage-giving answer. Jesus said:

Go back to John and tell him about the miracles you've seen me do—the blind people I've healed, and the lame people now walking without help, and the cured lepers, and the deaf who hear, and the dead raised to life; and tell him about my preaching the Good News to the poor. Then give him this message, "Blessed are those who don't doubt me."

MATTHEW 11:4-6, LB

What had Jesus done? He had sent John a message from the Book of Isaiah, from which they had both drawn much inspiration. In it Isaiah had spoken of the acts of the Messiah, and what Jesus said was virtually a direct quotation from Isaiah 35. Jesus wasn't lightening John's load but strengthening his back.

This is how Jesus handled a doubting John. He could have used the moment after the messengers left for a sermon at John's expense. Would he not have been justified in saying to the onlooking crowd who had witnessed this entire interchange, "It's a shame about John. I know he's in a tough place, but he's a good example to all of us about what happens when a man doubts. Don't be like him"?

But instead, Jesus' words to the crowd are, "Of all men ever born, none shines more brightly than John the Baptist" (v. 11, LB). At John's lowest moment of doubt, Jesus made a strong observation about his value. Jesus could handle John's doubts. They seemed neither to surprise nor upset him.

Such doubt was never a part of my earlier life. A well-loved child, I had never had problems trusting in anyone in authority over me. Being able to freely trust God was included in that gift. But there came a day during our dark months when I was forced to admit I had a colossal case of doubt. Scripture reading was difficult; praying by myself was a battle. There were hard questions deep down within me that I was afraid to acknowledge and ask.

Unconsciously, I had come to the conclusion that I knew what God would and would not do. But when the unthinkable happened, God would not be confined to my neat little box. His understanding is infinite—mine is finite. But it took a friend who had known me over twenty years, a friend who had earned the right to say hard things to me, to suggest the possibility of doubt. Once I was able to acknowledge my doubt and raise it to God, as John had done to Jesus, release and peace slowly returned.

Time to Reflect

Have you ever doubted God? What did you do with those doubts—have they been dealt with or smashed down? Ask God to give you a sense of his unconditional love so you can raise your doubts without fear. Trust God to lead you through them to a place of trust again.

Prayer for the Day

Father, sometimes my nerve endings seem frayed and my will weakened. Please come to me in the way you did to John and give me the sense that you are in this mess with me. Thank you for not berating him for his doubts. It gives me courage to bring mine to you.

Twenty

The Riveted Eye

Keep your eyes on Jesus, who both began and finished this race we're in. Study how he did it. Because he never lost sight of where he was headed—that exhilarating finish line in and with God—he could put up with anything along the way: cross, shame, whatever. And now he's there, in the place of honor, right alongside God. When you find yourselves flagging in your faith, go over that story again, item by item, that long litany of hostility he plowed through. That will shoot adrenaline into your souls!

HEBREWS 12:2-3, THE MESSAGE

One day while Gordon and I were resting from a long hike up a mountain pass in Switzerland, our reverie was broken when we heard the bark of a dog from the valley far below. Along the pathway below us came a farmer with a large dog following close on his heels. The two were headed toward a herd of brown cows that were scattered in the grass on either side of the alpine stream.

Our binoculars brought the scene closer. It was clear that the farmer intended to round up his cows and move them to another pasture. He and his dog would do the job together.

We were fascinated by what came next. The farmer simply pointed to a distant cow, and the dog instantly bounded off. As the dog approached the cow, it began frenziedly barking and nipping at the cow's hind legs. When the cow could abide the nuisance no longer, it began moving in the direction of the farmer. That caught the attention of other cows and soon they were all on the march.

The dog returned to the farmer when his task was completed. He crouched in front of him, tail wagging, eyes fixed, waiting for the slightest gesture that would send him off again on another assignment. The farmer and his dog performed perfectly as a team. Nothing impressed us as much as the dog's attentiveness to the wishes of his master. We were both amazed at what appeared to be the dog's single-mindedness as it would return again and again, sit, and wait for the next command.

We carried away that picture of the dog with his eyes on his master. It symbolized the kind of devotion we have come to learn must be given to the heavenly Master. And we prayed that afternoon for a similar "riveted eye" that waits for the Master's slightest gesture.

In contrast, I was reminded of another dog Gordon and I meet each day when we take our daily walk back at Peace Ledge. His name is Dunno. Apart from loudly barking at every passerby, Dunno seems worthless. He lies lazily in the sun until we are about twenty-five yards away and then explodes into noise. Until we are far out of sight he keeps on yapping. Then he lies down again and waits for the next walker.

They are two very different dogs. One begs his master for a chance to serve. The other begs people to bug off. One wags his tail in a burst of enthusiasm; the other seems to gripe and complain at the slightest disturbance.

Which am I, Lord? I asked as I silently pressed toward the top of the pass. *Am I a barking loafer? Or a devoted servant, anxious to serve you?*

Père Didon, well known for his work with children in the late nineteenth century, wrote to those who wanted to come and work alongside him:

I do not want people who come to me under certain reservations. In battle you need soldiers who fear nothing. Enlarge yourself then, and may noble sacrifices never appear to you too burdensome. Never say to yourself, "It is enough," but keep rising higher. Feelings are of very little value; the will is everything. God will not take you to task for your feelings, for it is not within the power of man to ward them off, or ally them. That which God looks at in the human soul is the will. The only thing that lies within our power is to will, to love.[10]

Time to Reflect

Where are your eyes today? Your Shepherd desires your closeness. Read Hebrews 12:2-3 again. Are you devoted enough to Christ today to obey him—no matter the cost?

Prayer for the Day

Father, I thank you that your eyes are always on me. I want to be alert, to obey your slightest command. Forgive those times when I've been too busy serving my own interests or fearing pain too much to follow your wishes. Impart courage into my soul, Lord. I'm learning the joy of your loving heart.

Section Three
❧

Courage to Find
the High Road

Each day of following Christ is an adventure that we can either endure or allow to bring zest and excitement to living. The thoughts in this section help us "test the waters" to discover for ourselves if we really believe what Christ said.

Keeping our attitudes and responses in line with the will of God is key to maintaining a healthy perspective on his call to walk the "high road." In this section, we will read about people whose lives were transformed because they chose to take God at his word.

Twenty-One

Being Careful Whom We Follow

He lifted me out of the pit of despair, out from the bog
and the mire, and set my feet on a hard, firm path and
steadied me as I walked along.

PSALM 40:2, LB

Corrie ten Boom, who was imprisoned for hiding her Jewish
neighbors during World War II, once said, "Never be
afraid to trust an unknown future to a known God." She lived
what she said. Losing her father and sister in the Holocaust
meant trusting the God she knew well for all the unknowns that
lay ahead. The above verse from Psalm 40 was true in her life.
And so it has been for Gordon and me.

There are aspects of my journey that I would not have chosen either, but in looking back, I see that God has literally
turned evil days into redemptive yeses. Book mentors like
Corrie and Amy Carmichael were my models for how to have
confidence in God during evil times. Amy did her best writing
and deepest trusting from her twenty years in bed—insisting
that her affliction bear lasting fruit. When I needed to find the
higher ground, such admonitions as the following helped me
obey the truth, no matter how I *felt*.

"Anything but that, Lord" had been your earnest prayer.
And then, perhaps quite suddenly, you found your feet set on
that way. Do you still hold fast to your faith that he makes

your way perfect? It does not look perfect. It looks like a road that has lost its sense of direction; a broken road, a wandering road, a strange mistake. And yet, either it is perfect or all you have believed crumbles like a rope of sand in your hands. There is no middle choice between faith and despair. Life is a journey; it is a climb; it is also always a war![1]

I never expected to be free of failures—mine or the defeats of those I love. What I hadn't prepared sufficiently for was public humiliation. Sometimes, it seems as if God says, "I'll make a spectacle of them and if they say yes to it, I will use this shameful time in spite of them!"

To accept such experiences freely has meant that I have had to keep the sufferings of Jesus as my straightedge. After all, I reminded myself, he was stripped naked and nailed to a cross, *in front of his mother!* Could I shrink from things he embraced for me? Hardly. Besides, *we* deserve our pain; he did not. We make choices that move us away from God's laws, but we cannot choose the consequences.

Perhaps you find yourself on a path that looks as if no good can come from it. The simple word *yes* makes all the difference. *Yes* to the humbling, *yes* to the deepening, *yes* to praying, *yes* to being quiet, *yes* to grace, *yes* to being stripped of externals, *yes* to unconditional love, *yes* to life! There must also be the nos—*no* to blaming others, *no* to becoming resentful, *no* to resisting truth, *no* to making excuses, *no* to comparing ourselves with others, and *no* to embracing hate or slander. Ruth Graham understands such moments when she writes:

Lord, when my soul is weary
and my heart is tired and sore,
and I have that failing feeling
that I can't take any more;
then let me know the freshening
found in simple childlike prayer;
when the kneeling soul knows surely
that a listening Lord is there.[2]

Time to Reflect

Are you willing to follow a Savior who bids you come and be humbled as he was? What do the thoughts from Amy Carmichael mean to you today? Do you believe that life is a journey and always a war? How would embracing these thoughts change your actions?

Prayer for the Day

Father, I know myself well enough to admit that when the heat is turned up I prefer the easy way out. In those moments, come and remind me of my need to follow in *your* footsteps. I want King David's words to be a reality in me, "When I called, you answered me; you made me bold and stouthearted" (Ps 138:3).

Twenty-Two
✥

Heroes of Our Faith

"You have said, 'It is futile to serve God. What did we gain by carrying out his requirements and going about like mourners before the Lord Almighty? But now we call the arrogant blessed. Certainly the evildoers prosper, and even those who challenge God escape.'"

Then those who feared the Lord talked with each other, and the Lord listened and heard. A scroll of remembrance was written in his presence concerning those who feared the Lord and honored his name.

"They will be mine," says the Lord Almighty, "in the day when I make up my treasured possession. I will spare them, just as in compassion a man spares his son who serves him. And you will again see the distinction between the righteous and the wicked, between those who serve God and those who do not."

MALACHI 3:14-18

Is it encouraging to know that others have struggled to take the high road, from the earliest of Bible times? People who continue to mark us are those who humbly lay down their lives for others.

One of the most humble persons Gordon and I ever met was Christy Wilson, who, along with his wife, Betty, served Christ and his people for many years in Afghanistan. As a pastor in the city of Kabul, Christy led his congregation in building a sanctuary. There came a time when the Wilsons were forced by the government to leave the country. They had no desire to leave, but circumstances beyond their control seemed to prevail; so their ministry in Kabul ended. Later, another command came to the church from the government: Abandon the new building, because it will be destroyed.

Gordon and I remember receiving a telegram from interested Christians that called on followers of the Lord throughout the world to pray for the protection of the church building. Thousands prayed for a miracle of deliverance for this place of worship. But God had another kind of deliverance in mind—a deliverance of the heart.

After the Wilsons had returned to the United States, word came that bulldozers belonging to the Afghan military had come to destroy the church property. Betty told a group of us later of their long waiting for news from Afghanistan and then of Christy's reaction when they learned that the building had been reduced to rubble.

He simply fell to his knees and gave thanks. Why give thanks? Because as the believers at Kabul met the soldiers and their heavy equipment at the church site, they served them tea and cookies while the soldiers undertook their mission of destruction. No wonder Dr. Wilson gave thanks.

They took the higher road. They might have whined and cried "foul"—how come those evil people are prospering, Lord, while our people have lost their place of worship? But their people had learned well how to be free to love their enemies—that was miracle enough. They said a resounding *yes!*

The prophet Malachi tells us that God is keeping records of such treasured possessions. Nothing we do in his name goes wasted, in the long view of eternity. Press on in this day to love and give without thought of return.

Time to Reflect

Which thoughts win out in your heart: "It's not fair," or, "I could also serve my enemies tea and cookies"? Dr. Wilson just recently went home to heaven. Who will the next generation of Christy Wilsons be? What about this story draws you higher?

Prayer for the Day

Lord, I see what these people did as an act of your grace on earth. Thank you for giving the inner strength to do such things with joy and unity. May I and the people with whom I live and worship be drawn to such sacrifice and death to selfishness.

Twenty-Three
&

Freeze-Frame or Video?

The Lord is compassionate and gracious; slow to anger,
abounding in love. He will not always accuse, nor will he
harbor his anger forever; he does not treat us as our sins
deserve or repay us according to our iniquities.

PSALM 103:8-10

In thirty-nine years of marriage, Gordon and I have accumulated thousands of feet of movie film and thousands more
photographs and slides of the great and small events in our lives.
Each of these visual reminders commemorates a moment in our
family history; there are yet more pictures to be taken in the
future.

When our children were teenagers, they were never eager to
see pictures of their childhood because they didn't want to be
identified with some of the embarrassments of the past. I've
come to appreciate that when any of us experience a major set-
back or failure, we feel much the same way. There are always
people in our lives who take us back to the former days and
show us old movies about our more infantile moments.

Similarly, when someone has failed us, it is all too tempting
to use that failure either as a club or as a barricade. With each
reminder of prior failure, our loved one is driven farther away,
making the restoration of the relationship less and less of a possibility. We may feel justified in our actions, for that person has

hurt us. However, these actions do not reflect the mercy of our loving Savior.

Thankfully, Christ does not remind us of our preceding failures. It's almost as if he says to us, "Life is not a photograph upon which your existence is frozen for all time; rather, it's like a movie or video; it continues on and on. Moment after moment—some sad, others grand. I didn't stop at your wayward moment and lock it in. I see your repentance and how you rebounded and went on to obey me. So let's move on to the next frame in the video and rejoice in your later growth."

Time to Reflect

In the scrapbook of your life, are there any pictures you would rather tear up and throw away? A hasty word, a thoughtless action, a hurtful remark that you would give anything to "do over"? Write down those experiences, and include the words of those who have hurt you the most. When you have finished, place your list in a fire-safe container and burn the list, praying the prayer below.

Prayer for the Day

Lord, I thank you that you see my life in process, as in a video, and in your great mercy forgive me for these sins. Help me to make amends toward those I have harmed. I entrust _____ into your hands, and ask you to help me to choose forgiveness toward this person so that I might continue my journey unhampered by resentment or bitterness. And even as I thank you for not locking me into past failures, I pray that you would give me the grace to not lock others into past wrongdoing either. Thank you for hearing my prayer.

Twenty-Four

When Someone Waits
in the Darkness With You

My soul is overwhelmed with sorrow to the point of death. Stay here and keep watch with me.... My Father, if it is possible, may this cup be taken from me. Yet not as I will but as you will.

MATTHEW 26:38-39

What did our Lord ask of his friends as he headed for those dreaded hours on the cross? Sympathy? Not really. Most of all, he seems to have wanted their companionship as he wrestled through the greatest of all temptations: the momentary desire to escape the suffering that was just ahead. He would have liked for them to have shared his prayer burden as he moved beyond the temptation and into the great statement of submission: "Thy will be done." Those who are able to do this for us are our best friends.

I recall one day in particular. It was one of the lowest days in my adult life. All the promises and the things I'd learned and taught seemed to slip away from me, just when I needed them most. I was unable to help myself climb out of a mood; a sense of despair and pessimism seemed to engulf me.

Miles away was a friend, a Presbyterian pastor, who had frequently phoned Gordon and me. He would often send books and articles through the mail to encourage and instruct us. When we had prayer needs, we had learned that he could be counted on for intercession, often specifically checking back until the need was met.

One night he was awakened soon after he had fallen asleep. The Spirit of God impressed upon him the need to intercede for Gail MacDonald. In obedience, he arose and did so, on and off all night. As he read promises in Scripture concerning hope, he read them with me in mind, and then he wrote them down and sent them to me the next day.

This friend had no way of knowing that I was fighting one of the great spiritual battles of my life that very night. And I had no way of knowing that he was praying. But the one thing I did know was that when I awakened the next day, the battle was over. The suffocating heaviness of the day before had been lifted, and new hope had taken its place. The difference between the two days was as extreme as I have ever experienced. But why had this liberation happened?

Three days later, our friend's letter with the written Scripture promises arrived, and then I understood at what cost I had gained a heart of hope. This friend had pointed me to the Sufficient One as he prayed, and as Jonathan did for David years before, he strengthened my hand in the Lord (see 1 Sm 23:16). I will always be thankful for this man, for his gift of a night's sleep, and for the care given to someone so far away.

Robert Raines tells of a young woman, the wife of an army officer, who found herself living in the midst of a western desert while her husband carried on military duties. Hating desert life, she wrote a letter to her father, complaining about the absence of vegetation and the general misery of desert life. He wrote back a simple old piece of poetry:

Two men looked out from prison bars;
The one saw mud; the other saw stars.

Thinking through the implications of such a simple couplet, she determined to make her desert prison a place to see the stars. She began to study desert life and went on to become one of the foremost experts on desert cacti.

Her father could have made things easier for his daughter by telling her she had every right to complain. He could have sent her a ticket and told her to come home. But he didn't. His comfort was in words of challenge. Sometimes we need someone to pray or to admonish us in order that we might get beyond a dark night of the soul and in so doing find the courage to seek the high road.

Time to Reflect

When was the last time you heard God's voice through the care of a friend or spiritual mentor? Or, just as significant, when was the last time you were such a comforter to someone else? We need to be comforters who point others to Christ; we also need to have one or two to comfort us if we are going to make it through the dark times standing firm. Name them and give thanks.

Prayer for the Day

Thank you, Lord Christ, for being willing to go through such utter agony in order that we can know we have a high priest who has suffered everything we have. Yours are truly loving, trustworthy, and everlasting arms. But I need to learn more about how to do this for others and also how to be willing to be comforted by others without shame.

Twenty-Five

Whatever Happened to Humility?

For out of the overflow of the heart the mouth speaks.

MATTHEW 12:34

Especially when we are going through confusing and troubling times, it is important to have friends and loved ones who will encourage us to rise above the vindictive sickness of this age in which the words *me* and *my* seem supreme. We can ill afford to get tangled up in it. To lower ourselves to such behavior is to risk losing our soul's health in the process. François Fénelon's words have often moved me:

> Let yourself be humbled; calm and silence under humiliation are a great benefit to the soul.... Do not get angry about what people say; let them talk while you try to do God's will. As to the will of men, you could never come to an end of satisfying it, nor is it worth the trouble. Silence, peace, and union with God ought to comfort you under whatever men falsely say. You must be friendly to them without counting on their friendship. They come and go; let them go—they are but as chaff scattered by the wind.[3]

Years ago, Bishop Whipple worked at being that kind of person when he said: "For thirty years I have tried to see the face of Christ in those with whom I differed." It takes humility to see the value of what seem to us to be the "far-out" opinions and values of others and how their views harm us. Each generation has faced this challenge. Pride is slow to die.

Time to Reflect

The Proverbs tell us "the tongue has the power of life and death" (18:21). If you find it difficult to restrain your mouth from saying everything you are thinking, you probably will have strained relationships. But the mouth often "prints" what we allow to stay in our hearts. Centering on the humility and self-control of Christ is the place of beginning again.

Prayer for the Day

Oh God of earth and altar
Bow down and hear our cry
Our earthly rulers falter
Our people drift and die.
The walls of gold entomb us
The swords of scorn divide
Take not your thunder from us
But take away our pride.

G.K. Chesterton

Twenty-Six

Contributing to Another's Joys

Your care for others is the measure of your greatness.

LUKE 9:48, LB

In my study of the sufferings of Jesus, I have been challenged to realize that his pain began long before the cross. The anticipation of what was ahead must have magnified his suffering greatly. Yet during that agonizing countdown toward Calvary, Jesus seems to have managed the stress by giving himself to others.

There is great genius to the notion that pain becomes more manageable when one becomes disciplined to contribute to the joy of others. This is among the toughest of disciplines, one that demands great tenacity of purpose. But it works! I've seen it work in the life of a woman I highly admired and loved.

My Aunt Georgia taught children who were disabled. Because she lived not far from my girlhood home, I saw her frequently. It saddens me now that as a young girl I took her for granted. When Aunt Georgia was alive, it never dawned on me to ask her why she had chosen the single life or why she had made a commitment to people who were disabled. Only long after I had left home, was married, and began to reappraise my family roots did I begin to uncover Aunt Georgia's unusual story of personal honor and valor.

Why was she single? The fact is Aunt Georgia was a widow. Georgia Scott had married Walter Dickens, a railroad train conductor, many years before I was born. After several months she became pregnant, and the two of them began to anticipate the birth of their first child.

The happy home they had envisioned was not to be; their baby died soon after birth. Then, while she was still in the hospital recovering from the delivery, Aunt Georgia was notified that Walter had been killed in a train accident.

How does one put life back together after a double blow of this magnitude? For my Aunt Georgia, the answer came in the pursuit of this principle: She determined to contribute joy to others. Some of the benefactors of that determination were my parents, then newly married. Instead of hoarding the home she and Walter had shared, she allowed my parents to buy her home with a no-interest loan—paying her back as they were able. Then she returned to school, majoring in special education, a relatively new discipline in public schooling. In my files I have her first teaching contract, which offered Aunt Georgia $750 a year to teach children who were disabled in the Aurora, Illinois, school district.

For the next thirty-five years, my aunt taught twenty children a year. When she retired, scores of people came to pay her honor. When I read the description of all those who praised this quiet, determined woman, I asked myself what the Aurora community would have done if my Aunt Georgia had rebelled against her pain instead of choosing to use it by contributing to the joy of others. This is the high road.

Time to Reflect

Someone wisely said that a contented person is one who enjoys the scenery along the detour. This is what Aunt Georgia did. Do you tend to choose the high road, as my aunt did? Think about the people in your life who have nurtured you as my aunt cared for me. If they are still alive, have you thanked them? If gone, are there relatives who could benefit from your reminder of how thankful you are for their heritage?

Prayer for the Day

Such thoughts buoy up my spirits, Lord. Thank you for the multitude of people over my lifetime who have contributed to my joy in the midst of their stresses and pain. Please bring the Aunt Georgias in my life to mind often. Too frequently they are passed over to get to my complaints. Father, I'm sorry, and grateful that with your help, I can choose not to repeat this pattern.

Twenty-Seven

The Pearl—A Wound Healed

"But I will restore you to health and heal your wounds,"
declares the Lord.... "I have loved you with an everlasting
love; I have drawn you with lovingkindness. I will build
you up again and you will be rebuilt."

JEREMIAH 30:17; 31:3-4

A pearl, I'm told, is a wound healed. No wound, no pearl.
Whether life grinds us or polishes us depends upon what
we are made of.

In her book *Thank You, Lord, for My Home,* Gigi Tchividjian
writes of a day when her mother, Ruth Bell Graham, visited the
shop of a man who specialized in piecing broken pottery and
china back together. It was Mrs. Graham's wish to buy something with one piece missing. When the craftsman showed surprise, she explained to him that his activity reminded her of
God's work in human life. "God," she said, "carefully and
lovingly takes the broken pieces of our lives and glues them back
together again."[4]

Here and there, all of us have missing pieces: a death, a
divorce, an illness, an injury due to someone else's wrongdoing.
Still, God glues us back together. The cracks and holes will
remain until some day in eternity, when they are restored to
their intended beauty. Even then, we are in his everlasting arms.

While we are putting the pieces back together, let's not forgo
the opportunities of today. Teresa Burleson puts this concern in

words so delicate and descriptive that I would suggest the reader scan the words three or four times before going any farther.

> We ponder God's withholding
> or bestowing
> And while we pine for what
> was never given,
> And what was taken,
> Today slips through our fingers.

Time to Reflect

It's easy when we feel wounded to dwell on and get stuck in the hurt rather than the beauty of the "pearl" coming out of it. For Jesus, the joy set before him was the "pearl." Think about this past week; have you been prone to waste the opportunities of the moment because you are dwelling too much on what may never be? Think on Jesus' commitment to you. Can you believe today that he wants to rebuild you with lovingkindness? Envision the fact that Scripture says Christ prays for us. Let hope fill you.

Prayer for the Day

Lord, I don't need to try to fool you; there's no fooling you. You know that today I'm not interested much in the pearl. I can't seem to get past the pain. Help me. Yes, I am forever thankful that Christ suffered so terribly for me—without complaint. But today that's head knowledge, not heart. Please be patient with me until I can move past this place to the place of healing and joy.

Twenty-Eight
❧

Staying on the High Road—What Helps?

When you come, bring the cloak that I left with Carpus at Troas, and my scrolls, especially the parchments.

2 TIMOTHY 4:13

A while back, a man wrote to us to say that the daily discipline of journaling had helped him immensely on his long walk away from drug addiction. This one-day-at-a-time struggle was encouraged as he came to his journal each day to deal with the truth about himself and his circumstances. Later when he returned to reread each entry he was encouraged to see change. He was learning to face the truth instead of blaming others for his problems and avoiding the person he had become.

Adoniram and Ann Judson left Salem, Massachusetts, to be missionaries on the subcontinent of Burma in early 1812. They lived without a home and traveled constantly for the first eighteen months. Ann had to adjust to living aboard several different ships, and the stress was enormous. But her habit of journaling became a powerful tool for reviving her inner strength. Finally on land for a few months, she wrote on May 6, 1813:

Have been distressed for some days, on account of the gloomy prospect before us. Everything respecting our little mission is involved in uncertainty. I find it hard to live by

95

faith, and confide entirely in God, when the way is dark before me. But if the way were plain and easy, where would be the room for confidence in God? Instead, then, of murmuring and complaining, let me rejoice and be thankful that my Heavenly Father compels me to trust in Him, by removing those things on which we are naturally inclined to lean.[5]

By writing out her thoughts, she could make them manageable. This discipline helped her in the earliest months of their adventure. As they boarded their ship to Rangoon, Burma, Ann was eight months pregnant. They had hired a European woman to help with the delivery. However, the woman fell to her death on the deck of the ship just before they sailed, leaving Ann without aid when her first child was born. Weeks later, when the baby arrived, it was stillborn. The Judson's second child died at the age of eight months.

For three years she and her husband received no mail from home. Nearly five years passed before they saw anyone confess Christ as Lord as a result of their ministry.

At one point, it became necessary for Adoniram to leave Ann in order to make a journey to Chittagong. They agreed that Ann should stay and manage the fledgling mission. Six months passed and Ann heard nothing from her husband. To complicate matters even further, the mission's very existence was threatened.

Cholera came to Rangoon, and rumors of war between England and Burma began to circulate. Was any of this affecting Adoniram? Ann was left to her imagination. She wrote in her journal:

How dark, how intricate the providence which now surrounds us! Yet it becomes us to be still and know that He is God, who has thus ordered our circumstances.... I know I am surrounded by dangers on every hand and expect to see much anxiety and distress; but at present I am tranquil and intend to pursue my studies as formerly, and leave the entire matter to God.[6]

After over six months' absence, Adoniram Judson returned following months of detours and storms that had sent his ship to India instead of home to Burma. How had Ann survived God used her ability to express her feelings on paper to keep her from losing her equilibrium. *She told herself not only how she felt but what she believed.* Both were essential to her survival.

Time to Reflect

Are there experiences in your life from which you might gain meaning if you were able to quantify their value and impact on you? Have you tried writing them down? Why not give it a try—begin small. Think about what Morton Kelsey said: "The journal is like a little island of rock on which we can stand and see the waves and storms for what they really are, and realize how hard it is to be objective when one is tossed by them."[7]

Prayer for the Day

Father, perhaps I need to try harder to put what you are saying to me on paper. I have no idea where I'll find the time for this. But I'm open. Help me to carve out time and give me the desire if this is something that would cause me to grow closer to you.

Twenty-Nine

Prayer—The Main Event

"Before they call I will answer; while they are still speaking
I will hear."

ISAIAH 65:24

C.S. Lewis once said that God goes everywhere incognito. All it takes is a moment to open our hearts to him—no matter where we are. We call this prayer—the connecting of our hearts and wills to God's divine purposes. These can be the highest thoughts we think. But it doesn't just happen.

Prayer is not trying to get God to do our will. In prayer, we *realign* our life desires, life purposes, and life plans to God's ways. E. Stanley Jones once used the analogy that the outcome of prayer is like a well-tuned violin, which will vibrate in unison with the piano with which it was tuned. When God strikes certain notes in his nature, we find our heartstrings vibrating in unison, provided prayer has attuned us.[8]

As a child, I can remember foolishly praying for a bike or something I wanted to serve my own selfish ends. But as I grew older, I found that the promise Jesus gave was for my daily *needs*—not my *wants*—and that my desires had to be brought into harmony with God's will, not mine.

Now I understand that to pray something in Jesus' name is to pray according to Jesus' character—he would approve of it; it squares with his will. In effect, I am saying, "I know his heart well enough to ask this." Understanding this has made many prayers die on my lips unuttered.

Furthermore, I've learned that being quiet and listening is far more important than my continual asking. My role is to consciously give as much of myself to God as I'm able at the moment. Lloyd Ogilvie states it so well:

> Prayer begins with God...(Is 65:24). It is not getting God's attention, but focusing our attention on Him and what He has to say to us.... It is a response to His call. We pray not so much to change, as to receive, the mind of God. He is able to impress His mind upon us.... Prayer gets us into the position of willingness to receive what God wants.... In the quiet, we begin to see things from His perspective and are given the power to wait for the unfolding plan of God.[9]

Fanny Crosby, who became blind when she was a child, told of a time in her adult life when she wrote the hymn "All the Way My Savior Leads Me." She needed five dollars and had no idea where she would get it. She prayed about it, and a few minutes later a stranger came to her door and handed her that exact amount.

Crosby was awed by God's care for her. "I have no way of accounting for this," she wrote, "except to believe that God, in answer to my prayer, put it into the heart of this good man to bring the money. My first thought was, 'It is so wonderful the way the Lord leads me.'"

Now, this is being attuned to the heart of God. Her life was one of outpouring and joy. She believed that God in his infinite mercy had used her blindness, "to consecrate me to the work that I am still permitted to do."[10]

Time to Reflect

Write down your first responses to this entry. What stands out as being most important? What would you say is your level of intimacy with God in prayer? Are you seeking to align your heart with his will, or are you primarily asking that your desires be met?

Prayer for the Day

Lord, I guess it's fair to say that prayer is not the "main event" for me—yet. I, like your disciples, need you to teach me to pray. I look at these thoughts and realize I'm missing out on something wonderful. Occasionally I get a glimpse of what might be possible if you and I were truly "attuned." It causes me to desire more.

Thirty
&ce;

Holding Everything Loosely

For I have learned to be content whatever the circumstances. I know what it is to be in need, and I know what
it is to have plenty. I have learned the secret of being content in any and every situation....I can do everything
through him who gives me strength.

PHILIPPIANS 4:11-13

From 1972 to 1984, Gordon and I spent twelve of the best
years of our lives in Lexington, Massachusetts, where he was
a pastor. When it became clear that it was time for us to leave,
it was hard for me because by nature, I am a rooted person.

In preparation for the good-byes I saw coming, I began what
I called a "move journal." The journal, I reasoned, would be a
place to deal with my feelings. I would record insights from
Scripture and other sources with the expectation that it would
prepare me for the trauma of the impending move. I wanted to
make sure that when Gordon resigned, he wouldn't find me to
be a drag on the momentum God was generating in leading us
to a new place.

During this same period, I had been developing a Bible study
for the women of our congregation concerning women in
Scripture. As always, what we do for others comes back to bless
us. My study disclosed an important lesson relevant to my

world. I saw that six women of the Bible who were major players in God's dealings with people—Eve, Sarah, Leah, Rebecca, Lot's wife, and Hannah—all faced one of two challenges. Either they were asked to leave their homes, or they passed through a time in their lives during which they were infertile.

Being highly sensitized to the first of these by experience and to the second through a number of friends who were dealing with infertility, I reflected on the amazing commonality these biblical women shared. It was as if early in God's relationship with women, he wanted them to understand that he was Lord of the "move" and Lord of the womb. Having created us, he understood the pain we might feel in both situations. To permit women to face insecurity in one or both of these areas is to challenge them at the very core of their lives.

I've picked up these same themes in the lives of some of my favorite mentors in Christian history. After five years of marriage and three children, Catherine Booth, wife of the founder of the Salvation Army, wrote to her parents: "It appears that God may have something very glorious in store for us, and when He has tried us, He will bring us forth as gold. My difficulty is in leaving home."[11]

Of the great missionary Mary Slessor, her biographer wrote:

On the night before she left home to go, not overseas, but only to Edinburgh for her course ... the woman who would one day be described as "a tornado" crept down to the door of the lobby of the tenement building where she lived and cried her eyes out.[12]

When Amy Carmichael prepared to leave England for Japan, where she had her first missionary experience, people thought her a hero. Only she seemed to know that she was in deep personal pain. She said, "They think I *want* to go. If they only knew how torn in two I feel today, and how precious the home ties are, they would understand...."

When I study biblical women and try to appreciate what their feelings must have been, I am comforted to know that God is not silent or unfeeling about them—or us. Like them, we are heard and we are understood. But this comfort comes only when God is given the title deed to our lives and permitted to take our pain and turn it into a growing experience.

Time to Reflect

When Ruth Graham was asked how she endured so many good-byes, she said, "Make the least of all that goes, and the most of all that comes." Can you do this? Has your relationship to Christ made all the difference in the necessary changes life has brought your way? If not, what one step can you take to trust God more?

Prayer for the Day

Father, I'm eager to take the high road in how I trust you in the "leavings" of people and possessions in my life. I want to hold on to people and things so loosely that when you say, "Go," I can do so with a ready spirit.

Section Four

Pathways to Forgiveness

The path toward forgiveness is one all of us must choose if we are to follow after Jesus, the One whose death makes forgiveness possible. I've tested these principles of forgiveness, not only in my life, but in the lives of many with whom I've walked through hard times in four decades.

No one needs God's loving arms more than one being called on to forgive or be forgiven. The act of forgiving one another is at the crux of every healthy relationship. In most situations, it's a God-sized task. As you read through this section, open your heart and be encouraged in the hope of restoration.

Thirty-One

ॐ

Removing Whatever Hinders

Let us strip off anything that slows us down or holds us
back, and especially those sins that wrap themselves so
tightly around our feet and trip us up; and let us run with
patience the particular race that God has set before us.

HEBREWS 12:1, LB

Gordon and I often go hiking in the mountains, whether
near our home in New Hampshire, in the Colorado
Rockies, or in the Swiss Alps. One thing we have learned over
the years about hiking is that the lighter the load, the more
delightful the walk. This realization causes us to ask ourselves
whether we have truly pared back to the bare essentials each
time we go walking. Do we need two cameras and all those
lenses? Is it wise to carry all that fruit? Will a sweater substitute
for a jacket?

The issue of carrying weights in the inner life is even more
important. Any number of things—guilt, despair, bitterness,
hardness against God, the need to prove oneself and win, jeal-
ousy, and envy—bog down the spirit, changing what could be
a delightful ascent in life to a disaster.

No heaviness in the spiritual dimension seems greater to me
than the weight of anger and resentment. If it isn't identified
and discarded, this "baggage" accumulates as time passes. This
causes the one carrying it to expend increasing amounts of

energy, for no good purpose.

Consider one woman who is deeply hurt by the betrayal of another and chooses *not* to forgive. In so doing, she effectively nails herself to that event in time, making future forward motion difficult. Another woman, however, knows a similar betrayal and chooses to manage the pain and hurt by giving mercy and forgiveness. She not only steadily moves beyond the event to further growth, but gains a bit more strength and resilience to become an even more forgiving person in the future. One act of grace-filled forgiveness usually begets another.

As our Western world becomes more comfortable in non-Christian lifestyles, and as spiritual warfare becomes increasingly vicious in the Christian community, most of us are going to face the need to forgive over and over again. A new generation coming into adulthood is no doubt going to have to learn how to forgive a parental generation it feels was too busy to give proper affection and affirmation. Women and men are going to have to learn how to forgive spouses who have succumbed to terrible temptations. Sooner or later, each one of us will undoubtedly face a major forgiveness moment with someone we love. The question is, are we preparing *now* for such a time by living a *lifestyle* of grace?

Grace was not easy for me to give or receive during the earliest years of our marriage. Being able to say I was sorry and owning my part in a conflict was difficult. Often Gordon would graciously take responsibility for things I should have, until *years* later, when I was willing to own my own frailty and culpability. Some of us never learn to say and mean those most important words, "Forgive me, I was wrong."

In many homes the wounds and hurts a family inflicts upon its members are never cleansed with words and actions of repentance; instead, wrongdoing is covered by a spirit of *niceness* that never gets to the root of the offense. However, doing something nice for the person we hurt doesn't cleanse the wound. Only the words "I'm sorry, it was my fault" (followed by actions that match the words), will do. If *niceness* instead of repentance goes on year after year, the layers of hurt build up into a glaring wall of resentment. These things don't just go away with time.

In this passage in Hebrews, the apostle Paul suggests that these unnecessary loads or walls of hardness are stripped away only through our willingness to proactively rid ourselves of them.

Time to Reflect

How heavy is the weight of resentment in your life? Have you honestly evaluated your part in an unhealthy relationship? Do the above words of the writer of the Book of Hebrews strike a chord in you today? Take the needed time to honestly face this possibility. Jesus is the freedom giver. Name it and ask for his help to embrace the process of forgiving.

Prayer for the Day

Lord, I know that I tend to keep myself too busy to even look at the amount of weight I am carrying with regard to people I need to forgive—to say nothing of those who need to forgive me. Help me open up the window of my soul to you so that you can rid me of those things keeping me from true freedom. Thank you for never giving up on my resistance to your work in my life. I yield to you today.

Thirty-Two

Putting on the Right Things

> Clothe yourselves with compassion, kindness, humility, gentleness, and patience. Bear with each other and forgive whatever grievances you may have against one another. Forgive as the Lord forgave you. And over all these virtues put on love, which binds them all together in perfect unity.
>
> COLOSSIANS 3:12-14

We do not learn to forgive in the hour of crisis; rather, we train for forgiveness in our better moments. Does it sound strange to say that in our best moments we prepare for the worst ones? In this case, we study the meanings of forgiveness and how it is portrayed in Scripture. We watch and learn from others who are going through situations needing forgiveness. And we monitor our own spirits to observe our progress in times of small irritations or conflict. Are we instinctively vindictive or easily drawn to give grace?

Forgiveness is at the heart of our faith. The cross stands in bold relief as the most magnificent example of giving grace in the face of sheer meanness and hardness of heart. To honestly be able to say with our Savior, "Father, forgive them, they don't know what they are doing," is the ultimate freedom.

Just as we *strip off* the attitudes that are harmful, we must proactively *put on* or *clothe* ourselves with the fruits of his Spirit, which are life-giving and sustaining. It is helpful to see how Paul mastered this. He never forgot that he was, before anything else, a forgiven man. Forgiveness was a gift he'd received from God, then from the church—though he had been responsible for the incarceration, murder, and scattering of many Christians. Looking back on those days, he wrote of himself: "I was once a blasphemer and a persecutor and a violent man." And then he goes on to add: "I was shown mercy…. The grace of our Lord was poured out on me" (1 Tm 1:13-14).

Later, when it was Paul's turn to suffer in various towns and villages where hostile people turned on him, he must have frequently said to himself, "Now I experience what I once did to other followers of Christ. What if the Lord had poured upon me the vengeance I deserved rather than the grace and forgiveness I needed?" This man who had formerly been so hardened and vindictive became gracious and kind, refusing to fight back at those who attempted to make his life so miserable.

Paul's refusal to be hostile to his enemies reminds me of a comment Andrew Murray's daughter made about Andrew after he suffered terribly from injustice. His experience was enough to have turned many of us into bitter cynics. But Andrew was different. When his daughter was asked how suffering had affected her father, she replied, "It has left him unable to think an unkind thought of anyone."

One wonders how suffering might have affected Paul *had he not* developed the instinct of a forgiving spirit. What if, instead, he had chosen to carry the accumulated weight of hatred for those who threw stones, arranged for his beatings, tried to discredit him, left him for dead? Here is one who has much to teach us.

Time to Reflect

Do you hold grudges easily? Is it difficult to let go of hard feelings toward one who has offended you? Are there those with whom it would be difficult to sit down and pray because you harbor hostilities toward them? Running from these realities isn't the answer. The attitudes we "put on" are important. Even if others never take off the wrong attitudes and put on the right ones, we can.

Prayer for the Day

Lord, please help me to let go of my hostility and forgive as you have forgiven me. I know I am responsible for only my own behavior and heart attitudes, but I need to remember your words of forgiveness and the words of people like Andrew Murray. Enlarge my heart to receive such power from you and then to give you praise.

Thirty-Three
ɘ৮

Resentment Could Have Ruled Him

[Love] is not rude, it is not self-seeking, it is not easily angered, it *keeps no record of wrongs.*

1 CORINTHIANS 13:5, EMPHASIS MINE

What happened in the tiny mountain town of Lystra is the first good example of what we can learn from Paul. There, a murderous mob stoned Paul, dragged him outside the city, and left him for dead (see Acts 14:19). When he recovered, he went on. But while most of us would have avoided that city like the plague, Paul later returned. Why? Because he held nothing against those who had thrown the stones.

The result? He met a young man named Timothy who became like a son to him and carried on his apostolic ministry long after the old apostle was gone. Timothy would never have become Paul's protégé if a hardened, bitter spirit had caused Paul to stay away from Lystra—the place of the stones.

The cruel stones unerring fell upon him—
Until they deemed his bleeding form was dead;
His worth and work they knew not, and they cared not;
Enough, they madly hated what he said.

God touched him! and he rose, with new life given;
Nor in his bosom burned resentful pain;
And, by and by, when need and call both guided,

113

He to the stoning-place returned again.

Perchance you too have tasted cruel stoning—
And might be glad if call came ne'er again
To turn to scenes where surely there awaits you
The cruel, cutting stones which make life vain.

Yet, if "back to the stones" the Finger points,
Then you shall know there is no better way;
And there, just there, shall matchless grace await you
And God Himself shall be your strength and stay.

J. Danson Smith[1]

Paul's proactive choice to take off hate and put on love—not once but over and over again—was the seedbed for many transforming events in his life and in the lives of others. The late Dr. Karl Menninger once said, "Love cures people—both the ones who give it and the ones who receive it." He understood, like Paul, that a daily choice to love makes the difference. In our world the operating *system* is vengeance, but, thankfully, we can choose a better way.

John Perkins, the former leader of *The Voice of Calvary* in Mendenhall, Mississippi, went through inhuman beatings during the years when racial violence was at its worst in our country. At first he found himself hating those who had "stoned" him, and he wanted revenge. But as he lay in the hospital bed, recovering, the Holy Spirit reminded him of many Scriptures having to do with the power of forgiveness. He finally *heard it* and said to Jesus, "I forgive them, too."

Perkins went on, "I promised the Lord that I would return good for evil, not evil for evil, and then he gave me the love I knew I would need to fulfill His command to 'love your enemy.'"[2] John and his wife, Vera Mae, returned to the place of the stoning and spread years of love, and have continued to for decades since.

Time to Reflect

Think about a "stoning" time in your own life. Have you worked past the need to get even and found freedom within? Or are you stuck? What need in your life is being met by holding on to this? Write your thoughts, and pray that God will help you choose love over resentment.

Prayer for the Day

Lord, I recognize I am far more complex than I'd like to admit, but I desire to be free and to free others. I truly do not desire to hang on to the wrongs people have done to me. I know you are the only one who can empower me to act, so I'm casting myself on your mercy today. Please begin this work in me, Father.

Thirty-Four

🪶

Developing the Instinct

> The jailer woke up, and when he saw the prison doors open, he drew his sword and was about to kill himself because he thought the prisoners had escaped. But Paul shouted, *"Don't harm yourself! We are all here!"*
>
> ACTS 16:27-28, EMPHASIS MINE

Paul responded admirably a second time when he was pitched into a jail at Philippi (see Acts 16:23). Stripped and beaten, he and his companion, Silas, were placed in an inner cell, their feet fastened in chains. It appears that the jailer had maximized their discomfort before going to his own comfortable bed. It could have been a time for Paul and Silas to decry the injustices of those who had jailed them and to plot the vengeance they were going to bring down on the town's authorities on their day in court.

But that wasn't the way they chose. The two men prayed and sang in worship until about midnight, when there was an earthquake. The jailer awakened and quickly decided to take his own life, assuming that a vengeful Paul would have escaped.

But Paul's *inner conditioning* once again surfaced. Instinctively, his concern was for the jailer—this man who slept through the apostle's misery; this man who had more than likely either enjoyed Paul's earlier beating or made it happen himself; this man who had offered no medical treatment or suit-

116

able comforts.

"Don't harm yourself!" Paul cried out. Would we have responded this way? Would it not have been easy to say, "Let the man do anything he wants to himself; he has it coming"? We may not seek to cause direct harm to another, but we might not mind if our enemy harms himself. Isn't that what the expression "Let him hang himself" really means? Paul's soul instinct was such that he not only refused to harm the jailer directly but also prepared to intervene if the jailer sought to "hang himself." Forgiveness was set in motion *before* it was asked for.

In this story, everyone wins. The jailer and his household become believers. Paul and Silas have their wounds dressed and are fed and welcomed into the jailer's home as friends. Question: Would the letter Paul later wrote to the young church at Philippi mean what it does to us today if Paul had not been the gracious man he was that night?

But wait. Sandwiched between the story of Lystra, which we looked at in the last chapter, and Philippi is a third incident, this one about an unforgiving, seemingly implacable Paul. I wonder if Luke highlighted it there with a lesson in mind for readers like you and me.

John Mark became a point of contention between Paul and his one-time companion, Barnabas. Earlier, Mark had shown himself unable to endure the rigors of the first apostolic journey and had turned back toward home (see Acts 15:37-40). Later, Barnabas was willing to overlook that failure and give Mark a second chance; Paul was not. The two men disagreed so strongly about the matter that they parted ways.

Imagine how Paul must have felt later when he realized what his impulsive temper and unwillingness to show grace to Mark had cost him. Now he was estranged from his dear friend Barnabas, who had been the only one willing to take a great risk to bring Paul into the church in the earliest days of Paul's faith. When Paul had been given the chance to give much the same kind of grace to Mark, he had failed.

Later, Paul would change his mind about Mark and make note of him as a highly profitable partner in ministry (see 2 Tm 4:11). The Bible gives no indication of a connection, but I have often wondered if Paul's eager, forgiving response in Philippi is partly the result of his having processed the harsh, severe lesson of his failure with Mark and Barnabas. Whether or not this is so, we see Paul as a man who drains each experience of all he can learn so that the power of the cross is seen in him.

Time to Reflect

Think about this story and the good that came from it. Are there times when evil things were done to you, but God meant them to train you toward a grace-giving response? Reflect on ways you think God may be using "jail-like" events in your life for inner conditioning. How have you responded? Pray for insight and courage to change your soul instinct.

Prayer for the Day

Thank you, Father, for the way you have graciously turned the evil things I've offered up to you into something good. Would you grow this powerful, life-giving instinct in me today? I recognize my total inability to do this without your power changing me from the inside out.

Thirty-Five
❧

How Paul Learned to Forgive

Be ... tender-hearted, forgiving each other, as God in
Christ also has forgiven you.

EPHESIANS 4:32, NAS

Who taught Paul to be tenderhearted and forgiving to others when he faced such terrible opposition both from unbelievers and, sometimes, from people who called themselves believers? From where did his practice and instinct of forgiveness come?

Did it start with what he saw in the life of Stephen on the day Paul gave consent to the man's death? What did it mean to Paul when he heard the dying Stephen pray words similar to Christ's, "Lord, do not hold this sin against them" (Acts 7:60)? That brief prayer must have banged about in Paul's soul for a long time afterward.

Paul may have learned from Stephen that what happens to us when people hurt us won't matter years from now *unless* we have chosen to carry the resentful memory of it like a dead weight through life.

Was Paul's education in the art of forgiveness also a product of his experience in the city of Damascus, soon after he had received the heavenly vision of Christ on the approach road? Blinded and weakened, Paul (then Saul) must have been overwhelmed when Ananias—a prophet who had every reason to fear and resent Saul of Tarsus because of his murderous reputation—entered the room, laid hands on him, and said, "Brother Saul."

Think of it! Paul must have expected anger—or at least a lecture. But instead, with the touch of his hands came the affirmation that things done in the past would not deter him from receiving the grace of God. Paul was a *brother!* What Stephen had started, Ananias continued, and Barnabas later sealed.

Knowing of the command of Jesus to "produce fruit in keeping with repentance" (Mt 3:8), these men became a lifeline to Paul, who needed to see forgiveness lived out. Later, he would write of the mandate he received from Jesus. "I am sending you to them to open their eyes and turn them from darkness to light, and from the power of Satan to God, *so that they may receive forgiveness of sins...*" (Acts 26:18, emphasis mine). Having learned it well, Paul preached that "they should repent and turn to God and *prove their repentance by their deeds*" (v. 20, emphasis mine).

When our children were three and six, we hosted a unique musical family when the Singing Murks gave a concert for our congregation. The parents and their five children traveled continually in a large bus, yet maintained a closeness that amazed us. Fortunately, they parked their bus in our driveway, so I had several days to see how they related to each other.

After watching the amazing way these small children got along, I asked Mrs. Murk how she taught them to be so forgiving. She told me that building and forgiving had always been a top priority in her teaching of the children when they were small. If she found them to be in conflict, she would get them to look one another in the eye and quote Ephesians 4:32 (NAS): "Be kind to one another, tender-hearted, forgiving each other, as God in Christ also has forgiven you."

They were then to hug each other and say, "I'm sorry; I was wrong." The Murk children became expert peacemakers among themselves and among their friends at school. Our family was so impressed by what they taught us that we resolved to make it work in our home. And indeed it *has!* Now we are in the second generation of children who lead in desiring to give and receive forgiveness.

Time to Reflect

Think about the rippling effect of Stephen's grace toward Paul. Can you remember a time when you were forgiven by someone before you repented of any wrongdoing? What did it do to you? Have you applied that experience to your own grace-giving opportunities?

Prayer for the Day

I'm thankful, Father, for Stephen, Barnabas, and Ananias, all of whom showed Paul the freedom there is in forgiveness. I want to embrace such heart attitudes too. Give me the grace to say, "I'm sorry," instead of laboring under a pride that insists that I "appear" right. Show me times when it is my turn to give the grace I have received.

Thirty-Six

Step One: Receive Forgiveness Myself

If I had cherished sin in my heart, the Lord would not have listened; but God has surely listened and heard my voice in prayer. Praise be to God, who has not rejected my prayer or withheld his love from me!

PSALM 66:18-20

Over the years, I have spent much time thinking through what the process of forgiveness looks like in personal relationships. It is not a once-and-for-all response. Forgiving is hard work, a supernatural work, and often emotionally draining. At times one feels the need to begin all over again, back at square one. And what is square one?

Because we can't give to others what we haven't received ourselves, forgiveness must begin with God forgiving us. Until I embrace the fact that *I* am in deep need of forgiveness, I will falter in my ability to give it to another. I addressed how I came to this moment in my own life in the first section of this devotional.

Jesus told the story of two brothers, both of whom needed forgiveness (see Lk 15:11-32). Since my own humbling experience, I've come to a new appreciation of the ramifications of this story. Whether one needs forgiveness for being a prodigal or for being unwilling to *forgive* a prodigal—either way, both can be captives to self-centeredness and need forgiveness. Seeing a person as a captive to evil rather than as our enemy is an important distinction. God has given us the privilege of helping to free captives.

The famous elder brother—whose welcome to the Prodigal hardly matched that of his father—was a kind of prisoner. He was as captive to his self-righteousness as his younger brother had been to the debauched lifestyle of the far-off country. He was, in fact, lost in his father's home! He was busy working for his father but was totally out of sympathy with his father's heart. As a result, the elder brother was unable to place true value on his younger brother. Blindness to pride made him unable to rejoice in the forgiveness offered to his brother.

No wonder the elder brother was so miserable when he heard the shouts of laughter at the welcome-home party given for his repentant sibling. I was startled when I heard someone ask the question, "What would have happened if the Prodigal Son, on his way back home, had met the elder brother first instead of his father?" Horrors!

The bottom line of Jesus' story suggests that *both* sons had actually drifted from the center, the place of their father's love. For the younger, the drift had been dramatic and hostile; for the other, the drift had been subtle, covered with "good flesh." For any of us, the drift can be either way.

When people choose to carry the weight of anger and resentment rather than a forgiving spirit, they run a serious risk. Paul put it this way when he admonished the Corinthians to forgive a man guilty of sexual sin who had openly repented: "A further reason for forgiveness is to keep from being outsmarted by Satan; for we know what he is trying to do" (2 Cor 2:11, LB).

Gordon and I have suggested to men and women whose repentant spouse had been unfaithful that a different but nonetheless destructive captivitity was in store for them if they refused to forgive. The enemy of our souls doesn't care *how* he destroys relationships, as long as they are destroyed. He is soundly defeated when we are able to receive God's forgiveness, which frees us to become forgiving toward others.

Time to Reflect

Are you willing to come to the Father and receive forgiveness for being self-centered? All of us have to enter his presence with this as our first plea. When we see our own fallen nature, we will then be able to understand the need others have to be forgiven. Until then, we will tend to feel superior. Visualize yourself free of guilt.

Prayer for the Day

I'm so grateful, Father, that you were waiting for the Prodigal with open arms. This is remarkable and comforting to me today. Whenever I am unwilling to begin with me, remind me that I must first come to you as a sinner and yield my life up to you. I come just as I am to experience your love and forgiveness, Lord.

Thirty-Seven

Step Two:
Recognize and Name the Offense

> Her brother Absalom said to her, "Has that Amnon, your
> brother, been with you? Be quiet now, my sister; he is your
> brother. Don't take this thing to heart." And Tamar lived
> in her brother Absalom's house, a desolate woman....
> Absalom never said a word to Amnon, either good or bad;
> he hated Amnon because he had disgraced his sister
> Tamar.
>
> 2 SAMUEL 13:20, 22

Before we can begin the process of healing forgiveness, we
have to recognize our hurt and name it for what it is.
Someone has said that demons love to go unnamed, and that
we can't change what we can't name. Maybe that's why Jesus
always appears to have named or identified demons, sins, and
inner attitudes that others would have liked to keep hidden.

It's easy to deceive ourselves and pretend we aren't angry, or
to think that if we let things be, adverse feelings will simply go
away. They won't. For a while we may be able to outrun them.
But they return. The spiritual cancers of resentment, hostility,
and vindictiveness require treatment. But before they can be
treated, they have to be brought to the physician who special-
izes in that field and be labeled.

In the Older Testament there is a very sad story involving the
rape of Tamar by her brother Amnon. Even though Absalom
was infuriated, he didn't talk about it, nor did he encourage

Tamar to speak of it. For years their father, King David, swept the betrayal under the rug.

There came a day when Absalom's rage boiled over and he gave orders to have Amnon killed. The killing mushroomed into more denial and unnamed hurts between David and Absalom, until one day Absalom revolted and overturned his father's kingdom. If David had helped his sons and daughter name the offense and deal honestly with it, years of messed-up living could have been avoided.

A woman I know, like many with whom I have visited or corresponded, confided that her father had sexually abused her as a young girl. My friend had successfully jammed all of her feelings and anger down deep into her soul, and for a long time she assumed that what had happened could simply be forgotten, like a bad dream.

But later that became impossible—especially when she married and began to face difficulties in sexual intimacy with her husband. It was not hard to find a connection between the struggles she was having in adult intimacy and the abuse of her past. In order to begin to heal, she had to acknowledge the betrayal and abuse of her childhood. Actions had to be named; feelings had to be identified; consequences had to be faced. Committing herself to the care of a competent counselor, my friend found healing for her wounds. In the process she learned the lesson of recognition and naming.

There is a universal reality for people who have experienced deep personal hurt at the hands of another—a parent, spouse, friend, relative, or working associate. Until the issue is fully defined, its effects will not be brought under control. But it's important that when we "unearth the garbage" we don't stay there but move on, lest we begin to smell like it!

When I converse with people like my friend, I challenge them with questions: Exactly what are we talking about? What feelings have been churning deep within you? When are you most likely to feel anger about this? What inhibition has it brought to your life? Are there certain types of people who naturally raise hostility in you, and what does that mean? These are *naming* questions, and they lead a hurting person to recognize truths deep within.

Time to Reflect

Are you aware of the unnamed, unforgiven offenses in your life that hold like a vise grip to your soul? Do you, with the help of a present Christ, have the courage to face them with a friend, pastor, or counselor? Think about it. Then take action toward healing.

Prayer for the Day

Lord, I know you are the great freer of captive hearts. Help me name those things that are dogging me and rendering me impotent to love others freely.

Thank you, Father, for giving me the courage I need today to take the first steps toward being unencumbered.

Thirty-Eight

Step Three: Resolve to Forgive ...
Over and Over Again

Then Peter came to Jesus and asked, "Lord, how many
times shall I forgive my brother when he sins against me?
Up to seven times?" Jesus answered, "I tell you, not seven
times, but seventy-seven times."

MATTHEW 18:21-22

Recently I spoke to a woman who had lost her husband
because of a misdiagnosis of an illness. Even though he
had died ten years before, she was immediately reduced to tears
when I said, "The holidays must be especially difficult for you."

She was surprised how close to the surface her tears still were.
She said, "Where did that come from? I thought I was through
grieving and forgiving the circumstances that surrounded his
death."

I have heard those words from different "forgivers" many
times over forty years of ministry. "Just when I think I've forgiven him, a tidal wave of anger comes over me, and I am once
again engulfed in feelings so intense I wonder if I've come any
distance at all!"

It's important to understand the intricacies of our inner lives
as they come to bear in the *process* of forgiving. After receiving
God's mercy for ourselves and naming the offense done to us,
we enter into what can be a lengthy period of resolving to forgive, over and over again. The length of time this takes depends

on the severity of the wrong done, the depth of the emotions, and the will to forgive. One thing is for sure: Our will to forgive must take precedence over our feelings.

Gordon and I have known people for whom the past, with its hurts and injustices, is as real today as it was twenty or thirty years ago when the original transgression occurred: A business-man angry at a former partner who cheated him; a spouse who has never forgiven the other partner in a sad divorce; a young person who bitterly resents a father too busy to pay attention to him.

Such people leave a significant chunk of their lives behind them, fastened to the unresolved event. They literally nail them-selves to the day that they refused to forgive. They are rarely free to hope. This is bondage. This is captivity. To resolve to forgive out of obedience to God is an unavoidable *starting point*. We think we are doing it for the other person but find to our sur-prise that *we* are the ones who are also freed from a horrible bondage that affects body, mind, and soul.

I remember when Gordon and I lived in New York City and our twelfth-floor apartment overlooked the East River. One day Gordon, who sees a sermon illustration in everything, pointed to the Empire State Building at a distance and said, "People are like that building: You look at that massive structure and think that it is a unit, but as you get closer you discover that there are over eighty floors, and on every floor something different is happening. No floor is necessarily aware of what is happening on another, and none of the activities are integrated.

"People are like that," he continued. "Stand at a distance from them, and they look 'together,' but the closer you get, the more you realize they are often in inner conflict with them-selves, and while 'Floor 50' has clearly gotten the message that forgiveness has been offered, 'Floor 38' sabotages them as though little or no forgiveness were given. The job of the for-giver is to get all of the floors in agreement."

It was a helpful thought for my grieving friend, whose life had been forever altered. The expected presence of her hus-band, the longing to share experiences with him as before, the realization that this didn't need to have happened, all of these things make the healing more difficult. But as she learns to be more patient with the complexity of the process, the healing comes.

Time to Reflect

Have there been times in your recent past when you were sur-prised at some emotion that returned when you thought it was forgiven? Does it help to think of yourself as far more complex than you once had thought you were? Christ may be Lord of all, but it may take us time to "feel" it in certain areas of life. That's why we need to be careful not to let our feelings rule us.

Prayer for the Day

Father, how great is your heart. So often I like to think of myself as quite simple to figure out. How I kid myself. But you know me through and through. I want to be able to have the will and hunger to forgive and forgive and forgive again. Keep me from getting stuck in past hurts. Again, I acknowledge my depen-dence on you for the abundant grace I'll need to follow through on this.

Thirty-Nine

Step Four:
Renounce Vengeance

Do not repay anyone evil for evil.... If it is possible, as far as it depends on you, live at peace with everyone. Do not take revenge, my friends, but leave room for God's wrath, for it is written: "It is mine to avenge; I will repay," says the Lord. On the contrary: "If your enemy is hungry, feed him; if he is thirsty, give him something to drink. In doing this, you will heap burning coals on his head." Do not be overcome by evil, but overcome evil with good.

ROMANS 12:17-21

L et's be frank. A person who has been deeply hurt may wish to hurt back. To be greatly offended is to feel rejected, devalued, humiliated—in some cases, betrayed.

The normal human reaction to such feelings is to make the offender experience the same feelings, so he or she knows what we have endured. We want to punish and inflict an equal amount of pain. The innermost parts of our lives can be very dark and mysterious places, and the instinct to return cruelty for cruelty dwells deep within us.

Not all of us are tempted to display overt vindictiveness. We may take pride in the fact that we are not directly striking back at someone who has hurt us. At the same time, we find ourselves delighting in circumstances where that person looks bad before others. Or we manufacture clever words and observations that put the squeeze on. Sometimes, acting wounded or innocent, we can find insidious ways to permit or even cause the other to be further humiliated or disadvantaged. We convince ourselves that we are not deliberately causing these things, but a brutal honesty would force us to admit that we are indeed driven by the desire to punish.

Forgiveness demands we renounce these desires. This is a spiritual work, requiring determination and often—at least for a while—an hour-by-hour choice. At times the only helpful motivation is to see Christ on the cross making the same choice. Jesus didn't fight his tormentors; he didn't rail against those directing the crucifixion. "Father, forgive them, for they do not know what they are doing" (Lk 23:34).

There is nothing quite so painful as being hurt by those closest to us. Even in this, we can follow our Lord's example. Jesus demonstrated real love and concern for his disciples, who had deserted him in his hour of need. And despite the fact that Peter had betrayed Christ, at no time did Jesus make Peter squirm or face public humiliation. He knew that Peter had suffered enough from the consequences of his actions. So when the risen Christ sent the disciples word of his resurrection, he saw to it that Peter received the message personally (see Mk 16:7). And on the shore of Galilee, Jesus made it clear to Peter that the shameful events of previous days were not to be remembered, that the commission given earlier was still in force. "Feed my sheep" (Jn 21:17).

All of this leads me to conclude that I need to be very careful that I do not take upon myself the role of judge and executioner when someone has sinned against God or against me. No matter how much something not made of God in us would like to do that at times, who of us can afford to put *our* souls in such jeopardy?

Time to Reflect

Refusing to exact vengeance for wrongdoing takes courage. Can you think of a time in your life when someone refused to avenge himself (or herself) against you? If so, what did it mean to you? Or perhaps there was a time when the opposite was true and you avenged yourself. What has that done to your soul?

Prayer for the Day

Lord, I find this one hardest of all. Surely the apostle Paul must have fought not being vengeful during his years of mistreatment, yet the words from Romans cut me to the heart. I need to make an exchange, Jesus—your tenderness for my hostility.

Forty
&

Step Five:
Covering

He who covers over an offense promotes love, but whoever repeats the matter separates close friends.

PROVERBS 17:9

From the life of King David comes a fifth milestone in the
forgiveness process. David understood that forgiveness
meant covering another's sin. That's a dramatic leap beyond
renunciation of vengeance.

King Saul's pursuit of young David through the wilderness
must have exhausted the bodies and spirits of both men. It went
on for *ten* years. The king's mood vacillations made it impossible for David to know what to expect next. One moment he
was being invited to be entertained at the palace; the next, he
found himself dodging spears and running for his life.

David's response was remarkable. Instead of throwing spears
back at the king, David chose to duck and simply leave his presence. We read of no vengeful words from David at these times,
only words of respect and sadness. One could argue that this
was an "unhealthy" covering—like the woman who "covers"
for her addicted husband who is unable to get out of bed and
go to work. A healthy covering does not hinder the natural consequences of bad choices.

If we look closely at the story, we see that David's actions were prompted not by an unhealthy desire to "cover over" Saul's wrongdoing but from a nobler motivation. David was determined not to be a source of trouble for God's anointed one, either by his words or by his actions. Even when David had a perfect chance to end the conflict between them by killing Saul, he restrained himself. He would not dishonor the man God had anointed ruler.

God saw to it that Saul experienced the consequences of his actions; Saul met a disgraceful death. Even then, David "covered" Saul with forgiveness. David could have seized the hour to exult in the king's demise as a vindication. In the thinking of many, he would have been justified in publicizing every single injustice, every betrayal, every sinister deed Saul had ever done to him.

But he didn't. He mourned the death of Saul (see 2 Sm 1:11-27). Moreover, he insisted that no one speak ill of Saul and that the nation honor him as much as they honored Jonathan. "Saul and Jonathan—in life they were loved and gracious, and in death they were not parted" (2 Sm 1:23).

We've all seen ourselves and others use innocent moments for vindictive purposes. It can be done quite skillfully—as a prayer request, as a testimony, as an item of "sharing" at a fellowship group. Few stop to realize that what sounds like a justifiable piece of information is really someone's way of venting anger or judgment. D.E. Hoste, once the director of the China Inland Mission, said, "Looking back over these fifty years, I really think that if I were asked to mention one thing which has done more harm and occasioned more sorrow and division in God's work than anything else, I should say talebearing."[3]

David chose the high road in his painful relationship with Saul. What others would have exposed, he covered. Could this be why David's son Solomon admonished that "love covers over all wrongs" (Prv 10:12)? In the New Testament, the only mention of David is that he was a man after God's own heart (see Acts 13:22). Did the Holy Spirit, who oversaw the writing of Scripture, make sure that David's most shameful choices and moral failures were covered in response to his gracious forgiveness?

Time to Reflect

How does the story of David and King Saul affect you? How does "covering" differ from "enabling" (in which the truth about another's irresponsible behavior is denied)? How is it less than full forgiveness when we don't cover? Consider times you've chosen to forgive—have you also gone on to cover the sin?

Prayer for the Day

Lord, please give me the wisdom to know the difference between healthy and unhealthy covering, and between true forgiveness and passive resentment. Prompt me with your Holy Spirit to recognize those times when I fail to "cover" another person's sins as I would want that person to cover mine.

Forty-One

Step Six:
Rebuilding

> Then Joseph said to his brothers ... "Do not be distressed
> and do not be angry with yourselves for selling me here,
> because it was to save lives that God sent me ahead of
> you....You shall live in the region of Goshen and be near
> me—you, your children and grandchildren, your flocks
> and herds, and all you have. I will provide for you there."
>
> GENESIS 45:4-5, 10-11

The sixth and final step in the process of shedding the need-
less weight of resentment and anger is rebuilding. This
means that, whenever possible, the forgiver needs not only to
cover the wrong but also to help the offender rebuild his or her
life. Deep remorse produces a kind of "spiritual limp," the sorrow a repentant person feels when he or she recalls the offense.
It becomes the forgiver's job to help lessen the limp.

Joseph suffered many kinds of adversity because of his brothers' choice to sell him into slavery. Joseph must have gone
through enormous temptations to feel bitter and vengeful
toward them. I've often wondered if he did not while away
many idle hours pondering what he would say and do if he ever
had a chance to meet up with them again. But God used
Joseph's captivity—as both a slave and a prisoner—to grind all

potential bitterness out of him. These were the years in which Joseph was learning the instincts of a leader—and the instincts of a forgiver. When Joseph left that dungeon to become one of the most powerful men in the world, he was a free man, unencumbered by pettiness, anger, or vindictiveness. He had given himself the gift of forgiving his brothers.

A careful reading of the biography of Joseph in the Book of Genesis suggests that the brothers, on the other hand, lived in spiritual bondage and guilt over their hateful act. Their guilt surfaced immediately when they came to Egypt to purchase food during a famine and appeared before Joseph, unaware that he was their long-rejected brother.

When Joseph and his brothers finally visited together, Joseph had both the power and the motive to be hateful and vengeful. He was in a position legally and had the right, according to the world's view of things, to hurt the brothers badly in return for what they'd done to him.

But he didn't. Later, in an emotionally wrenching meeting, Joseph disclosed his identity to them, acknowledged his long-worked-through forgiveness toward them, and even made note that God had taken their act and squeezed good out of it. But what he did then shows that his forgiveness was complete. He wanted to take care of them and nurture their young. This was rebuilding love.

All the principles I've noted in preceding pages play themselves out in Joseph's life: He *received* God's mercy in his own life, *recognized* and named the offense, *resolved* to forgive, *renounced* getting even, *covered* their sin, and *rebuilt* the relationship. All the steps are here.

In my life, these have been the steps to the joyous freedom that comes from releasing those who have harmed me. I know it to be a supernatural work of the Holy Spirit. Nothing less will do.

Time to Reflect

As you think about situations in which you've struggled to forgive someone, think specifically of what it would look like for you to be a "rebuilder" in those relationships. Now move backward in the noted steps, find where you're "blocked" in each situation, and take action to move forward toward this vision of "rebuilding."

Prayer for the Day

Father, thank you for seeing to it that Joseph's story is in Scripture. I long to be as free as he became. I'll admit that I'd like to take a shortcut, though. Take the coward out of me, Lord, and give me your relentless love that won't quit until rebuilding is complete.

Forty-Two

A True Story of Forgiving Love

Finally, all of you, live in harmony with one another; be sympathetic, love as brothers, be compassionate and humble. Do not repay evil with evil or insult with insult, but with blessing, because to this you were called so that you may inherit a blessing.

1 PETER 3:8-9

Years ago *Reader's Digest* told the story of Edith Taylor, who lived in Waltham, Massachusetts. Mrs. Taylor's husband had held a construction job that took him overseas to Okinawa after World War II. The two had agreed that, for economic reasons, it was best that she remain at home.

Months of separation passed, marked by almost daily letters. But as time went on, the letters from Okinawa came less and less frequently. Then one day a letter arrived that changed Edith Taylor's life forever. Her husband wanted a divorce. He'd met a young Asian woman whom he wished to marry.

Sadly, Edith agreed to the divorce, asking only that her husband be in touch with her occasionally so that she would know something of the direction of his new life. He promised he would.

Some years passed. Edith's former husband fathered two daughters with his Japanese wife. As the announcement of each birth came, Edith would send a greeting and a gift. Then one day a sad letter arrived. Mr. Taylor was terminally ill. Instinctively, Edith wrote to him to assure him that after his death she would do anything necessary to look after the welfare of his Asian family.

After her former husband's funeral, Edith invited his two daughters to come to America to live with her, since their mother was financially unable to care for them. But when the daughters came, it soon became clear that the separation of mother and daughters was unbearable. So within a few months, Edith Taylor made it possible for their mother to join them. In the years that followed, both women and the two daughters shared a home in Waltham. Edith had given herself the gift of forgiving someone else, and that generous act of mercy came back to bless the rest of her life.[4]

Time to Reflect

Occasionally we hear about a love that seems to walk right out of the New Testament. Can you think of anyone in your acquaintance who has loved as unconditionally and thoroughly as Mrs. Taylor? What character traits do you see in this person that enable him or her to forgive?

Prayer for the Day

Lord, I'm convinced of the power and necessity of a more forgiving heart. I desire to walk toward those who have wronged me in a whole new way—even if they aren't willing to walk toward me. It doesn't matter. You have shown me that I'm responsible only for my own heart attitude. Thank you for showing me so many things, Father.

Section Five

&

Hitting Your Stride

Someone has rightly noted that the problem with the Christian life is that it's so *daily*. To "hit our stride" in this faith journey, we must exercise various disciplines to maintain a heart of love for God.

For instance, sometimes it's helpful to examine *why* we're running the race of faith. What is it that pushes us to keep pace? Are we motivated by a sense of purpose? This section challenges us to take an honest look at the complexity of human nature and reveals the value of silence and solitude.

Forty-Three
֍

Seeking God's Pleasure

All this is for your benefit, so that the grace that is reaching more and more people may cause thanksgiving to overflow to the glory of God.

2 CORINTHIANS 4:15

When long-distance runners launch into the race, they speak of that moment when they "hit their stride." It doesn't happen instantly; in fact it may even take a while. But inevitably the runner reaches that moment when proper pace, conditioning, and mental attitude are all in balance. There is a sense that one could go on forever.

Listen to the winner after the race ends. "I knew I had the race won when I hit my stride." And the loser? "I don't know what happened today. I never quite hit my stride."

Eric Liddell, whose story we know from the movie *Chariots of Fire*, thrilled to the moment when he hit his stride. "When I run," he told his sister, Jenny, "I feel God's pleasure."

Now, there's an appropriate description for the spiritual journey or race (if you prefer that word picture). Hitting stride and feeling God's pleasure. I often have the sense that I'm in stride and feeling God's pleasure when I'm at worship and singing with unbounded joy. I feel it when I'm given the opportunity to encourage someone or to be used to lift a downhearted spirit. I have that sense when we open our home to guests, and I have the chance to practice hospitality in the name of Jesus.

I've been working on my "stride" for over forty years now,

and I've learned that when you hit your stride, you become lost in the notion of pleasing God and pleasing him alone. In that moment, you come close to forgetting yourself and how you appear to others. Gaining applause or credit becomes inconsequential. Worrying about what others think ceases.

You are what you are, and you do what you do to bring praise and pleasure to God—this is first and foremost.

Hitting stride, as the athletes say, doesn't happen overnight. It demands a lot of practice. The runner works on his or her posture, on the length of step, on the use of the arms and the positioning of the head. Countless hours are invested in building up the right combinations of leg and arm muscles. Then there is conditioning: the miles run, daily straightaway sprints so that the body develops endurance. Some would say that the mind itself must be conditioned so that its ability to persevere will not collapse when fatigue sets in.

But when race day comes, all that work, often done in secret, comes together. The starter's gun sounds, the runners leave their marks, and soon some of them "hit their stride." And it is the best of those strides that usually wins: the stride that doesn't capitulate to discouragement, to intense competition, to adverse circumstances; the stride that draws upon all the practice and all the planning that happened before the race.

As the Christ-follower makes his or her journey with the Lord over the years, a wonderful thing can happen. Take my word for it: life does not get easier; it may, in fact, even get more difficult. But the hesitant steps, the reckless steps, the foolish steps of the first days in his presence do give way to confident, assured, and purposeful steps. Sooner or later, if one has been faithful to the practice, the Christ-follower hits his or her stride and feels God's pleasure.

Time to Reflect

Think about what it would mean for you to "hit your stride." When do you feel God's pleasure? Are you willing to be patient with the process and the years it will take? Is the thought of bringing praise to Christ fixed in your mind as being more important than bringing praise to yourself? Ask the Lord to show you what brings him pleasure.

Prayer for the Day

Father, I'm grateful that you have a long-term commitment to making me more like Jesus. Help me to remember the patience of Christ, as Paul reminded the church at Thessalonica. Too often I want all of this today. I renounce impatience and I trust you with my today, desiring only that you teach me to trust you for each day's needs and always, always point me to Jesus, your Son.

Forty-Four

Potato Chip Choices

> Does not wisdom call out?... "Listen, for I have worthy things to say; I open my lips to speak what is right....Choose my instruction instead of silver, knowledge rather than choice gold, for wisdom is more precious than rubies, and nothing you desire can compare with her."
>
> PROVERBS 8:1,6,10-11

A friend returned to the United States after spending four years in a developing country. "What has been your biggest shock in reentering our culture?" I asked her.

"Walking down the potato chip aisle in the supermarket," she answered. At first I laughed because on the surface her comment did not seem profound or insightful. But she went on:

> The potato chip aisle is symbolic of everything our family is facing on this visit home. Four years ago when I went shopping, there were only a few varieties of chips on the shelf. Now I am faced with more choices than I have time for. Do I want potato chips that are plain or rippled? Fat-free, unsalted, or "fully loaded"? Barbecue, nacho cheese, jalapeño, or cheddar? It's unbelievable! I'm almost paralyzed with indecision. All I wanted was a simple little *potato chip.*
>
> *Why,* I ask myself, *should I spend important minutes in life deciding what kind of potato chip I'm going to buy?*

What a difference my friend's insight has made in my life! "Potato chip choices," I call them—those times when one gets inundated by insignificant choices and decisions. We are bombarded by the persuasive voices of those who call for our time, our loyalties, and our resources. Although their objectives are often noble, they seize a part of us before we have made any effort to discover what God wants.

Without a strong sense of purpose within us, our lives bang about like the ball in a pinball machine, controlled by those who create purpose for us. This tendency is magnified during times of crisis, when even small decisions can seem overwhelming. During the times we urgently seek God's direction and guidance, it is especially important to spend our resources wisely and to guard carefully the moments that are otherwise eaten up by the trivial and mundane.

Time to Reflect

What "potato chip choices" have you been facing lately? A certain amount of life is in the details, but if your primary focus is on choices that are ultimately of no real consequence, you will soon feel fragmented and worn out. If there are important decisions facing you right now, simplify your life so that you'll have more time and energy to seek a heart of wisdom. What are some practical adjustments you can make right away?

Prayer for the Day

Lord, may each choice I make today please you—both in what I choose and in how much time and energy I spend making my decision. Help me to be a good steward of my time and resources, so that I may gain a heart of wisdom.

Forty-Five

Living by Purpose

Since the day we heard about you, we have not stopped
praying for you and asking God to fill you with the knowledge of his will through all spiritual wisdom and understanding. And we pray this in order that you may live a life
worthy of the Lord and may please him in every way:
bearing fruit in every good work, growing in the knowledge of God, being strengthened with all power according to his glorious might so that you may have great
endurance and patience.

COLOSSIANS 1:9-11

When Beverly Sills was a child, she dreamed of being an
opera star. Nevertheless, she hated to practice. Each day
her parents had to prod her. Finally, exasperated, one of them
said, "Beverly, you need to learn to like what you love."

Sometimes you and I do not like what we *say* we love because
we aren't clear enough in the purpose and daily fleshing out of
that which is our passion. Where these matters become fuzzy,
less-than-best alternatives are likely to interfere.

Purpose-driven persons move through their days with an
economy of action. They know how to conserve their energy
for the important issues. These are people who allocate their
time—knowing how to say no and when to say yes. Purpose-
driven people don't panic in the face of setbacks and frustration;

they persevere in times of opposition; and they are not easily seduced by the flatterer or dissuaded by the critic.

A friend of mine defined her purpose with two simple words: "Choose life." For her, that succinct affirmation from the Book of Deuteronomy meant that whenever she had a choice to make, the life-giving solution was the one that would help her make up her mind.

"We can eat a candy bar or an apple," she said, "but which leads to a greater quality of health? We can watch TV or read a book, but which leads to a greater quality of growth? We can say a loving word or the critical word, but which conveys the quality of personal nourishment?" And so she chose to drive her purpose—a vital, healthy, growth-oriented life—through every action in the day. Ultimately, her purpose is to help others choose life as well, life as Christ offers it.

Time to Reflect

Do you carry a sense of purpose into every day? Use these thoughts to begin formulating a personal mission statement. Is there anything in your life right now that you need to relinquish in order to be able to better live out your mission statement? If so, what are you going to do about it?

Prayer for the Day

Lord, thank you for your many gifts to me. Help me to be a wise steward of those gifts, so that I might better fulfill your plans for me. May I be single-minded in my purpose and live in a way that brings glory and honor to your name.

Forty-Six

Sharpening the Blade—
It's Part of the Work

Come with me by yourselves to a quiet place and get some
rest.

MARK 6:31

One summer afternoon Gordon and I stopped to watch a
Swiss farmer and his wife cut mountain grasses for har-
vesting. Both swung large scythes from side to side with the
seemingly effortless grace of ballet dancers. After a time, the
"dance" stopped. The couple took sharpening stones out of
their pockets and, with the same agility, began sweeping the
stones back and forth along the curved blades of their scythes,
restoring razor-like sharpness to their tools.

As we pondered the couple's use of precious working time to
apply the whetstone to their blades, we realized that this pause
in the grass cutting was not an interruption of their work. It was
part of their work. Each cut was easier, each move more effi-
cient, because of the sharpened blade.

If you are like me, the verse "be still and know that I am
God" (Ps 46:10) is a personal challenge. *Doing* good things—
doing for and encouraging others—these *actions* often drive us.
But living off our natural energies will one day wear thin. If we
don't pause to "sharpen" our heart's devotion to Christ, we will
regress in our ability to "do." It's as simple as that. Inner

strength rekindled or sharpened before attempting exterior activity is part of Christ being formed in us. He did it; we follow in his steps. This becomes even more important when the heart is devastated by life's troubles.

Anne Morrow Lindbergh, although not necessarily writing from a Christian perspective, nevertheless has an intuitive grasp of this truth when she calls for a turning inward:

> Woman must be the pioneer in this turning inward for strength. In a sense she has always been the pioneer. Less able, until the last generation, to escape into outward activities, the very limitations of her life forced her to look inward. And from looking inward she gained an inner strength which man in his outward active life did not as often find. But in our recent efforts to emancipate ourselves, to prove ourselves the equal of man, we have, naturally enough perhaps, been drawn into competing with him in his outward activities, to the neglect of our own inner springs. Why have we been seduced into abandoning this timeless inner strength of woman for the temporal outer strength of man?[1]

In order to draw and give the life-giving water to others, we must first drink deeply of the springs of life ourselves. We must "come apart" in order to actively listen to God's inner whisper. For those of us who must plan everything—including the neglect of distracting *doing*—this represents a kind of *planned neglect*. Whenever Gordon or I have moved out of this rhythm of coming away from people to work on our relationship to Christ, we have regretted it later. By operating out of an *empty soul*, we miss out on the full experience of living in his everlasting arms.

Time to Reflect

Amy Carmichael observed, "Too much of your nature is exposed to the winds that blow on it. Do you need to withdraw more and more into the secret place?" Where in your day or week has there been any "planned neglect"? What one step might you take in that direction?

Prayer for the Day

Lord, all of these truths look so right on paper, but you know me and how much of my life seems a race to the finish. Forgive my neglect of things that matter to you. Be free to speak into my heart about these things today.

Forty-Seven

Uncovering Our Inner Resistors

Lord, you have searched me and you know me.... Before a word is on my tongue you know it completely.... Search me, O God, and know my heart; test me and know my anxious thoughts. See if there is any offensive way in me, and lead me in the way everlasting.

PSALM 139:1, 4, 23-24

There is something paradoxical in our experience of spiritual life. We say that we long to know God and to find strength and stability in his presence. Yet we are surprised to discover that another part of us resists that closeness, actually seems to want to flee his presence. Whatever could be the explanation for this reluctance? I can think of several possibilities.

One possibility could be a fear of spiritual failure. We've all known that high experience of a few days when it seems as if every moment is marked with his nearness. At such a time we may be tempted to think that we have reached a new level of spirituality and that, from now on, it will always be this way. But then, for reasons hard to comprehend, our progress is halted. We feel as if we are back where we started. And we become reticent to reach again.

Another possibility. We are sometimes seized with the notion that life needs more practicality, that prayer, Bible reading, reflection, and spiritual listening—while admirable pursuits—do not yield results fast enough, specific enough, desirable enough. Once again we hear an outer world saying that rushing about, shouting louder, and acquiring more are the real answer to life's challenges.

A third possibility. Some of us have learned that coming closer to God often means facing new and revealing truths about ourselves. This was Isaiah's experience. Brought into the presence of the glorious God, he suddenly cried out, "Woe is me!" In contrast to God's righteousness, he saw more of his own sinfulness. This is not necessarily an attractive thought.

Having worked with each of these possibilities more than once, I must tell you that I am most acquainted with this one. Since Gordon and I travel a lot, I am quite familiar with the fluorescent lighting often found in hotel bathrooms. When I look at myself in the mirror, the light amplifies the pits and flaws of my facial skin. True, I need this moment before the mirror to make myself presentable, but, frankly, there is a part of me that would prefer to avoid the truth the mirror ruthlessly reveals.

That can also happen as I push myself to seek God wholeheartedly. As I choose to move toward him, I cannot avoid seeing myself from a new perspective. Sometimes this can be a troubling moment if I am not quick to remember his grace and his desire to cleanse and change the pits and flaws of my heart.

If there is a fourth possibility as to why we might be less anxious to draw near to God, it could be that we know too many people who seem to be doing quite well without him. At least that is what it *looks* like. We ask ourselves, why try so hard if others are not trying at all?

I have decided that I cannot take my cues from them. Perhaps they confuse God's patience and *mercy* with his *approval*. So I fix my eyes upon the great men and women of

Scripture and of the larger family of God. I recall that they moved toward God at all costs, even if they were the only one in their generation. Then I tell myself that I prefer to line up with them than to line up with those who have found it convenient not to bother.

Some time ago, Gordon and I went through a period of humiliation in which we learned a most important lesson. The many years in which we had made it a daily practice to seek his presence made all the difference in how we were able to handle the consequences of failure. The disciplines developed in the good times sustained us in the bad times.

In his little book, *Shadows on the Wall,* F.W. Boreham suggests that everything in life attempts to draw us away from God, whom he visualizes as the divine Anchor.

> Every wind is against the anchor. The ship will go around with the wind, and the strain on the cable (which ties the ship to the anchor) is the same whether north, south, east, or west. Riches, poverty, success, or failure—they all put a strain on the cable.[2]

Yes, there is something paradoxical about spiritual life. We must never be surprised or confused about it. Though the prevailing winds of life might attempt to push us away, we must resolve on a daily basis that, at all costs, we will proactively stay close to the heart of God.

Time to Reflect

Some will ask, how come you failed if you were doing these things that were supposed to keep your souls? Good question. Nothing is fail-safe. But, when we get off the track, if these disciplines are in place, the rebounding is far more speedy as one rediscovers the track of obedience more quickly. Are they in place for you today?

Prayer for the Day

Lord, I open my life to you; let me see earth through heaven's perspective. Remind me, Holy Spirit, that you have made me to need to obey the laws and rhythms of creation. I want to welcome the convicting work of your Spirit, not fight it.

Forty-Eight
&

Snatching Chance Moments

This is what the Lord says—your Redeemer, the Holy One of Israel: "I am the Lord your God, who teaches you what is best for you, who directs you in the way you should go. If only you had paid attention to my commands, your peace would have been like a river, your righteousness like the waves of the sea."

ISAIAH 48:17-18

At this point in the book, you may agree with what you've read and acknowledge your need to spend "sharpening moments" with God. Yet you're stymied by two things: where to begin, and how to squeeze any more time out of your day. It's difficult, I know. Young mothers have babies demanding constant attention. Women working outside the home rush around, trying to juggle the many demands of home, work, and church. Women in mid-life must balance a host of responsibilities and obligations, often trying to meet the needs of both older and younger generations.

Every one of us has more than enough reasons to avoid getting started, but no matter how busy we are, we can still experience God's presence throughout the day. And when we are bruised and in need of healing, it is our communion with God that will sustain us.

Since my husband and I spend a lot of time on airplanes,

many of our best thoughts come to us there. One day Gordon pointed to the flight attendant coming down the aisle pouring coffee for passengers. "Note how she does it," he said.

I watched as the young woman asked each person to put his or her cup on the tray. Only then would she pour the coffee. "I suspect she does it that way," I said to Gordon, "so that if there is a bump in the air, she won't run the risk of spilling on anyone."

"You're right," Gordon said. "It's the same way with us. We must put our cup 'on the tray' if it's going to be filled by the Spirit of God. We must have the appropriate posture. God awaits my heart's willingness; he will not replenish it unless it's placed 'on the tray.'"

François Fénelon wrote a series of letters to a busy duchess in 1689. A portion of one of those letters sounds as if he was writing to some of us:

You must learn, too, to make good use of chance moments: when waiting for someone, when going from place to place, or when in society where to be a good listener is all that is required; at such times it is easy to lift the heart to God, and thereby gain fresh strength for further duties. The less time one has, the more carefully it should be managed. If you wait for free, convenient seasons in which to fulfill real duties, you run the risk of waiting forever; specially in such a life as yours. No, make use of all chance moments.... One moment will suffice, to place yourself in God's presence to love and worship Him, to offer all you are doing or bearing, and to still all your heart's emotions at His feet.[3]

So, the busy life is not restricted to our generation. We must start slow and small. For instance, wedge out sharpening moments by rising fifteen minutes early; grab ten minutes from a lunch hour; focus on your devotion to Christ during a late-afternoon commute on a bus or train, or in those never-ending traffic jams; use a thirty-minute period otherwise dedicated to television in the evening. Take fifteen minutes before bedtime. We must find time to place our empty hearts on his "tray" for filling.

Time to Reflect

Respond to this thought by the ancient philosopher Amiel:

> We must know how to put occupation aside, which does not mean that we must be idle. Inaction that is meditative and attentive smoothes away the wrinkles of the soul. The soul itself spreads, unfolds and springs afresh; and, like the trod-den grass of the roadside or the bruised leaf of a plant, repairs its injuries, becomes new, spontaneous, true, and original.[4]

How are your wrinkles?

Prayer for the Day

Lord, I am homesick for your presence. Having tasted it, I know what I'm missing. You know how often I feel as though I am drowning in obligations; though "good things," they can become an excuse to avoid time with you. You, Christ, the *more needed and necessary* person in my life, do not clamor for my attention, but lovingly wait for me to place my cup on your tray for filling. Help me take action on these truths today and find renewed joy in my relationship with you.

Forty-Nine
&

Coincidence or Provision?

My eyes are fixed on you, O Sovereign Lord....When my
spirit grows faint within me, it is you who know my way.
PSALM 141:8; 142:3

L ife's little details matter to God; all of creation reflects this.
When it was time to build the temple, God gave specific
instructions to the people of Israel, right down to the kind of
robes the priests wore. His instructions included minute details
most of us would argue don't matter. But they mattered to
God. He even told them to be sure that the neck on the robe
had seam binding around the edge to prevent the possibility of
fraying (see Ex 28:31-32).

When someone first shared that thought with me, I was
fascinated. Why was the God of heaven and earth thinking
about seam binding? Into my vocabulary crept a phrase, "seam-
binding moments," to describe those times when God seems to
orchestrate the tiniest circumstances for our benefit and growth.

We see this same detailed approach in Christ's instruction to
the disciples after he fed five thousand people. "Gather up the
crumbs and let nothing be wasted," he said. A seam-binding
moment.

We see it in creation. I remember when we visited the
Matterhorn in Switzerland. The guidebook informed us that
around the Matterhorn the local version of the common house-

fly comes equipped with "mittens and boots" (hairs in abundance), while in other climates, houseflies have no hairs. Call it a seam binder, reflecting God's attention to detail.

We see it in the direction God gives for the smallest things done in his name. An Ethiopian eunuch named Ebed-Melech is mentioned in Scripture because he did a kindness for Jeremiah the prophet (see Jer 38:7-13). Ebed-Melech influenced officials to release Jeremiah from a deep cistern where he was incarcerated. When it came time to pull him out, Ebed-Melech dropped rags down to Jeremiah to put under his armpits so that the ropes used to raise him would not burn him. The God of detail put it into the heart of one man to be concerned about another's armpits! Call it a seam-binding moment.

For two decades now I have kept records of seam-binding moments in my life. It causes me to stand in awe of a God who is specific.

Not long ago, Gordon and I were speaking at Bethel College and Seminary. We needed to get a photograph of Gordon to Switzerland the next day, but Federal Express told us the address we had was inadequate.

As we were greeting people afterward, a woman came up to us and handed Gordon her card. She explained that she had just been where he was going in Switzerland. Would he mind taking her card with a note on it to such-and-such a man? It turned out that it was the same man who was our contact person—she had his address! Furthermore, she was willing to take the photo to her home, scan it, and e-mail it to him that day! She called me late that evening to say that she had just heard from the people in Switzerland. The scan had arrived without a glitch. Amazing!

Our God desires to give us eyes that see *into* situations. He walks with us in the furnaces of life and gives grace and comfort that bystanders know nothing about. Too often the experiences reminding us that God knows our way are left to fray, lost in a morass of activity, because we don't take the time to reflect on them and write them down. Then we sadly miss the opportunity to see his love in his mastery of the detail.

Time to Reflect

Think about the last few days. Were there any "coincidences" that now you may see as God's kindness in your life? Write them down. Make it a fun practice throughout your day to look for the seam-binding moments, and see them as love notes to you from your heavenly Father. Give thanks.

Prayer for the Day

Father, I thank you that you show in Scripture that you care about the details of my life. Give me a heart to look for these serendipitous experiences, which will heighten my appreciation of your hand in my life.

Fifty
❧

Keeping Our Word

Now Moses was tending the flock of Jethro his father-in-law....There the angel of the Lord appeared to him in flames of fire from within a bush.

EXODUS 3:1-2

If you study the times when God appeared to his servants in Scripture, you will find that often he appeared to them when they were going about their daily routines and keeping commitments, even when it might have been inconvenient or seemed mundane to do so.

We first began to grasp this concept of keeping routines and commitments during graduate-school days. On one occasion, Gordon had promised a friend who pastored a small congregation of twenty-five people that he would preach for him at a Sunday worship service.

As the weekend approached, however, we had a crisis on our hands. We would have to vacate our apartment on Monday; we were forty-eight hours away from that moment with no place to go. Sunday was the last possible day to look around, so the temptation was great to call the pastor and tell him we would have to break our commitment.

Of course, it would be a major inconvenience for him because he and his family planned to be away that Sunday. He'd have to disappoint them or find another person to preach. But we also had an inconvenience on our hands. Wasn't it best to put our situation first?

No, we decided. It wasn't. It was our normal routine to worship on the Lord's Day, and usually we were busy in some sort of service—preaching, teaching, helping in the nursery, being with people. It didn't seem right to interrupt that routine even in the face of our perceived emergency. We had given our word. So we "bracketed," or put our crisis on the shelf for the moment and went to worship God.

Little did we know that among that small group was the answer to our prayers. After the service, I began to greet people. I noted a woman sitting in a wheelchair who had a quadriplegic disability. I was instantly drawn to her because she seemed a woman of cheer, a person who had obviously brought self-mastery to a very difficult lifestyle. After admiring her from a distance, I made my way over to greet her.

I was not disappointed. Immediately, she asked if Gordon and I could come to their home for lunch. I thanked her but declined. We had to grab a fast hamburger, I responded, because we had to find a place to live in the next few hours.

"You're kidding me," she said.

No, I informed her, I wasn't kidding.

"I may have the house you're looking for," she went on. She described a small home that her husband had just finished renovating: A house with a fenced-in-backyard (we had a two-year-old boy and a puppy); a house with a piano they'd like to leave in it (both Gordon and I play but had had no room for a piano); a house near shopping facilities (we had one vehicle); a house that was affordable (they would match the rent to our fiscal limitations); a house that came right from the hand of God, delivered by a woman in a small congregation that we had been tempted to avoid. We were only seeking an apartment, but God surprised us with a house!

That weekend we learned a powerful lesson and reaffirmed our "doctrine of the routine," which simply says: Do what you've prayerfully committed yourself to do, and let God vindicate your choice. Or, put another way, if you believe God has called you to certain convictions, certain responsibilities, certain relationships, maintain them at all costs before you turn to the more glittering alternatives that come out of the air. Then, look for how God will surprise you in the routines with his unmerited gifts.

Time to Reflect

Is keeping the routines or prior commitments important to you today? Think about your routines and the times that you have had to make a decision to honor them or choose an alternate option. How did you fare? Is there a need to revisit this in your life and fine-tune your thinking and doing? What gifts might you be missing that God has prepared for you along the way?

Prayer for the Day

Lord, this is a tough one for me, because I feel I do this commitment stuff all the time. When windows of opportunity come up, it's hard to embrace one more "ought to" in the face of a "want to." But I see now how you work through the routines and commitments to bring about your best in my life. Help me desire the bigger picture of your ways.

Fifty-One

The Power of Mood-Setting

Six days before the Passover, Jesus arrived at Bethany, where Lazarus lived, whom Jesus had raised from the dead. Here a dinner was given in Jesus' honor. Martha served, while Lazarus was among those reclining at the table with him. Then Mary took about a pint of pure nard, an expensive perfume; she poured it on Jesus' feet and wiped his feet with her hair. And the house was filled with the fragrance of perfume.

JOHN 12:1-3

In your imagination, put yourself in the middle of a candle shop or a Bath and Body Works store and recreate the smells and the ambiance there. Our entire mood can change when we enter a place where someone has taken the time to create an inviting atmosphere.

In the above Scripture, Mary did an amazing thing. She turned a dinner into a worship service. The focus went from the smell of food to the aroma of worship. Mary was practiced at drawing attention to Jesus, by sitting at his feet whenever we meet her in Scripture. This time was no exception. She was intent on what she was doing: It appears she was oblivious to what anyone else thought about her actions. Her objective was to honor her Lord, and if that offended the opinions and favors of others, it did not matter. She had one "Audience." She didn't nag or force others to join her; she acted on her own behalf.

And Jesus affirmed her—much to the surprise of those who wanted to criticize her.

It seemed like such a small thing to the others at the table. But Jesus said that Mary was the only one who got the picture—he was headed for the grave, through excruciating agony and loneliness. Mary's gesture of care would no doubt follow Jesus to the cross and, as others have noted, comfort him as the scent of expensive perfume lingered in his hair.

I cannot explain it, but I am aware that women have a subtle persuasiveness when it comes to mood-setting. A female distinctive through the ages has been the ability to intensify or diminish, direct, or redirect the moods of others. Women possess a "leverage" that can move others to higher—or lower—ground. They can choose to use this persuasiveness as Eve did, to derail good intentions, or as Esther did, to redeem bad situations.

Gordon often refers to me as the "emotional pendulum" of our home. He used to remind me that not infrequently both he and the children found it easy to pick up whatever mood I was projecting. Some could be offended by Gordon's comment. Some could say that's too much responsibility on my shoulders. I can think of a few times I tired of the accountability, but more often I saw it as a privilege.

I love what someone said about the English mother of Bishop Moule: "Her feet brought light into a room." Or the comment of a North African about Lilias Trotter, a gifted artist turned missionary, who spent her life loving, enjoying, and serving the Algerian people: "She was still and created stillness. She is beautiful to feel near. I love the quiet of her."

Most of us know about John Wesley, who in the eighteenth century founded Methodism, but we probably know relatively little about his hymn-writing brother, Charles. Professor David

Lyle Jeffrey, in a biographical account of Charles Wesley, says of him:

> His spiritual character was luminous, and communicated itself immediately to those who came into conversation with him. William Wilberforce … was captivated by Charles. He met him in 1786 in the house of Hanna More, and his later recollection of that encounter reveals something of the special presence of this unusual man: "… When I came into the room, Charles Wesley rose from the table, and coming forward to me, gave me solemnly his blessing. I was scarcely ever more affected. Such was the effect of his manner and appearance that it altogether overcame me, and I burst into tears, unable to restrain myself."[5]

Time to Reflect

Think back over the last two days. Were there mood setters in your world? Were they a benefit or a detriment to your experience? Think about a time when your mood influenced the mood of others. Did your mood help "derail good intentions" or "redeem bad situations"? What did you learn from this evaluation? Write some thoughts to solidify any conviction you feel at this moment, which will be a reminder for the future.

Prayer for the Day

Jesus, first of all, thank you for the way you honored this woman, Mary, when it must have cost you dearly with the others in the room. And thank you for times you have lifted me and reminded me of my value to you simply by who you are making me to be. Please help me in the days ahead to honor and thank those who are attempting to make life better for me by setting a mood of kindness or lightheartedness or hopefulness. And then, please teach me how to be one of them.

Fifty-Two

The Practice of Mood-Setting

> Every day they continued to meet together in the temple
> courts. They broke bread in their homes and ate together
> with glad and sincere hearts, praising God and enjoying
> the favor of all the people.
>
> ACTS 2:46-47

I love the thought that if we have a personal and vital relationship with Christ, others benefit from the Holy Spirit within us whenever we enter a room. It's a mood-setting for which we can't take credit.

Setting a mood at mealtime is one of my favorite activities. It's important that the people we love know we enjoy sitting regularly with them. Eating together is becoming a lost discipline with the frenetic schedules we keep, but it's a significant time for passing family values on to the next generation, and it's a wonderful way to stay connected to each other.

Today our adult children look back on our family experiences built around eating together and are most thankful. It was at the dinner table that we learned to talk and spur each other on to thinking more like Christ. The mood during eating was as important to me as what we ate. When the children were small, if they came into the kitchen with a bad attitude, they were kindly asked (and hopefully with humor) to leave the room and return only when they had a better one.

Placemats or a tablecloth (to cut down on noise), fresh flowers or colorful weeds (to add life to the table), and candles (to make us all feel valued) added a dimension of surprise to each evening. Sometimes, when we were eating leftovers that looked ghastly, I would turn off all the lights and use only candlelight. I called it "Italy Night" (with apologies to all Italians)! I assumed that I could pull any menu over on the family if I called it an exotic Italian dish.

Perhaps my love for mealtimes is one of the reasons Luke the physician is my favorite Gospel writer. It's Luke who often highlighted the routine of eating with others. Our Lord valued and made the most of the time he spent with people when they were disarmed by the enjoyment of food.

Gordon and I lived in Manhattan for several years. Even when eating out, we were proactive to create a mood of welcome and acceptance toward those we met in restaurants. Frequently after we thanked God for the food, a waiter or waitress would approach us and say he or she was a believer too, and that person took courage from our faith. We can set a mood anywhere, anytime!

We set a mood when we are willing to reach out and touch others. People must have physical touch to be healthy. Some people seem to require more than others. In fact, babies will die if they are not held. Scores of single people are starved for affectionate touch. And what of the many in marriages that have grown cold, where touching rarely happens? Gordon and I are frequently impressed with the number of couples with whom we visit where there is not the slightest hint of physical contact the entire time we are together.

Return to the story of Mary at the feet of Jesus. Her tender care toward his bruised and soiled feet was an act of gentleness and friendly affection. Some in the room were put off by her act. Jesus was comforted.

Somewhere I heard the story of a group of young medical students who were training in a large pediatric ward of a teaching hospital. As time passed, it was observed that one student was particularly loved by the children. Someone set out to discover why.

The student was followed through his rounds for an entire day. There seemed to be nothing exceptional about his routine, but in the evening, the mystery was solved. For as the lights were being turned out for the night in the various rooms, the student doctor managed to stop by the bedsides of all the children and give them a simple kiss good night. He was setting the mood for their sleep hours—a pocket of safety.

Time to Reflect

Think ahead to some upcoming opportunities where you can practice mood-setting with friends, family, or colleagues. What are some practical ways you will create a God-honoring mood in those settings? You may find it helpful to observe someone for whom mood-setting seems to be a natural instinct—learn by watching. Ask questions. And listen for God's prompting.

Prayer for the Day

Lord, I am challenged once again by the way you were willing to reach out to people who would one day turn on you. Sometimes I even find it difficult to show affection to people who have done a lot for me. Forgive me, Father, for withholding your love from others. Help me change this and enjoy being the vessel in which the Holy Spirit can deliver your enveloping character to others.

Section Six

৶৻

Living, Learning, and Passing It On

It is God's desire that every experience we come through be used one day to comfort someone else. Oswald Chambers once said that we should pay close attention when we are in the dark so we will have something meaningful to say when the light returns. If you are in crisis now, or ever have been, take heart as you read these thoughts on how God will one day use your situation to encourage others. And know, without a doubt, that all the while you are in his everlasting arms.

Fifty-Three

Kissed by Kindness

Be kind and compassionate to one another, forgiving each
other, just as in Christ God forgave you. Be imitators of
God, therefore, as dearly loved children and live a life of
love, just as Christ loved us and gave himself up for us as
a fragrant offering and sacrifice to God.

EPHESIANS 4:32–5:2

A merican artist Benjamin West used to tell friends that his
career was launched on a day in his childhood when his
busy mother asked him to take care of his younger sister, Sally.
Hoping to please his mother, Benjamin determined to surprise
her upon her return with a painting. He attempted a "portrait,"
he said, and the subject was his sister Sally.

As one might imagine, novice artists (in this case, a small boy)
are not exactly tidy about their efforts, and soon paint was splat-
tered everywhere. But when Mrs. West returned, she wisely
ignored the mess that would have sent most mothers into a tail-
spin. Instead, she focused only on her son's painting. "Why,
Benjamin, it's Sally!" And with those words she stooped down
and kissed her delighted boy on the cheek.

"That kiss," Benjamin later reflected, "made me a painter."

It's possible that Benjamin West's mother never remembered
the occasion and would have been surprised if anyone had told
her years later that such a simple, instinctive reaction had
empowered her son to pursue the artistic life. How often does
one make a substantial contribution in the life of another and

never realize its significance?

How many men and women in this world have desperately needed a word of grace, a comforting gesture, or an affirming touch and failed to receive it because those around them were not sensitive enough to realize how important it might be in a moment of failure or impending crisis?

No one is as sensitive as one who has been similarly afflicted. If you will allow it, your own thorny experiences can be transformed into a fragrant "love offering" to God—a bouquet of godly deeds and life-giving encouragement to those who need it most.

Time to Reflect

Is there someone in your life right now who needs your understanding and affirming touch? Someone who is currently going through a struggle similar to one you have already experienced? Think back to your own "dark hour." What gesture would you most have appreciated? Reach out to that other person—you have been uniquely gifted to share his or her pain.

Prayer for the Day

Lord, I am grateful for your faithfulness to me. Remind me of moments when I was in need of a lift and what that felt like. Make me a living expression of your faithful love to _____ today. May I be your eyes and ears and heart to this person in a meaningful way.

Fifty-Four

Listening to the Deep

When I felt secure, I said, "I will never be shaken." O Lord, when you favored me, you made my mountain stand firm; but when you hid your face, I was dismayed.

PSALM 30:6-7

I was an easy believer. If God said it, I believed it. And because of this, I had a tendency to put God in a neat little box—convinced he would not act outside of it. But one day he did. And I was devastated. It was not that I expected life without pain, but I was comfortable with the thought that following God's direction would keep me from experiencing the depth of consequence I now had to face.

It was a dangerous time. Thomas à Kempis once said, "Two things increase temptation's hold on us: an indecisive mind and little confidence in God." It took me quite a long time to admit that I was struggling with a colossal case of doubt. Scripture reading was difficult; praying by myself was a battle. There were hard questions deep within that I was afraid to recognize and address. But once I was able to acknowledge my distrust and lift it to God, I could get on with the *process* of rebuilding my confidence that God is *always* good, and he means to squeeze redemption out of everything.

This is why it has become increasingly important over the years to follow hard after people whose character and faith are deeper than mine—people for whom God's loving arms are assured. They don't have God in a neatly tied man-made box.

They leave room for mystery.

Eric Liddell faced all sorts of circumstances that at first made no sense. It is said that Eric had the most awkward running style of any athlete of his time. Ian Charleson, the actor who played Liddell in the film *Chariots of Fire,* said it was difficult to emulate his running style because he ran with his head back. When Charleson attempted it, he kept running off the track or bumping into other runners.

By the sixth day of filming, Charleson said he finally understood what Eric Liddell must have been doing. He recalled that in drama school he and others had engaged in trust exercises. They had run as hard as they could toward a wall, trusting someone to stop them. "I suddenly realized—Liddell must have run like that. He must have run with his head up and literally trusted to get there. He ran with faith. He didn't even look where he was going." What few know, however, is that Liddell stepped away from a great athletic career and the promise of a celebrity's lifestyle in England to become a missionary to China. Once there, he ended up in a Japanese concentration camp where he died at a relatively young age from a brain tumor.

Eric lived and died as he ran—with head up, trusting. His favorite words were "Absolute surrender" and "Be still, my soul." His final words to friends were simply, "It's complete surrender."

I am quite sure that Liddell would not have chosen to die in a prison camp at a young age. His children were not yet raised, and because of the war, he was away from his family. But he died peacefully, nevertheless. Why? Because he had a deep trust in Christ's long-term good for all things and he had surrendered his life to God's will.

Fénelon, who could have been Liddell's mentor in this matter of surrender, wrote: "If there is anything that is capable of setting the soul in a large place, it is absolute abandonment to God."[1]

These faithful ones and others were rare and treasured gifts to me. They helped me conclude that God would do with me whatever he chose. I would cease trying to write his script. My lack of trust had to be confessed and renounced. I was now willing to live by *every word* that came from God, not just the ones I could understand.

Time to Reflect

Perhaps, like me, you find it hard to own your doubts. Do you believe that God can handle them and love you without condition? You may find if you feed your faith, doubts seem to starve. Are you engaged with those who proactively go deeper or those who tend to enjoy the more shallow way? Do you think it really makes a difference to whom we listen? If so, what "voices" do you believe God would have you seek out in the future?

Prayer for the Day

Father, sometimes I want to go deeper, sometimes I hesitate. Surrender is a scary word, still I want to yield myself to your will. Teach me your truth as I listen to others who have gone deep and found you there. Let me learn from their wisdom that you are trustworthy.

Fifty-Five
&

Finding the Yes Behind Every No

For no matter how many promises God has made, they are "Yes" in Christ. And so through him the "Amen" is spoken by us to the glory of God.

2 CORINTHIANS 1:20

Two centuries ago, Englishman William Carey cultivated a dream to be an agricultural laborer. He loved gardening. But a skin ailment kept him from working in the fields, and he was finally forced to learn a new trade: shoemaking and repair.

The man who trained Carey in his new skill just "happened" to be a godly man who knew Greek. As the two men worked together, Carey not only learned the shoemaking trade, he also learned Greek from the Greek New Testament. In the process, Carey began to receive a vision for world evangelization. It was a case of an *initial no* leading to God's *ultimate yes,* for William Carey became the father of the modern Protestant missionary effort.

The death of Betsie ten Boom in a Nazi prison was a brutal *no* to Corrie, her sister, but it was the pathway to God's ultimate *yes:* The fleshing out of a forgiving heart for which Corrie ten Boom became known around the world.

When Joni Eareckson Tada was horribly injured in a diving accident, it was a glaring *no* to normal life, but God's ultimate *yes* has been the growth of a remarkable ministry to people who are disabled in our world. She has literally awakened the consciousness of the church universal to a ministry never taken seriously.

Linda, a friend of mine who is a ministry wife here in New England, was washing her clothes in the basement of her home when a man entered the cellar and, without a word, began to stab her until she fell virtually lifeless to the floor. Her husband was at a church meeting. When he returned home, he found Linda alive but unconscious. For days, her life hung in the balance.

To this day, the assailant has never been identified, but Linda has survived and returned to health. When people have said to her, "God was so good to have spared you," Linda replies, "God is good whether I lived or died." That has been God's ultimate *yes* to Linda. Her faith gained strength because of God's felt presence throughout her ordeal. Her faith has never been stronger.

The list goes on and on of people who have learned that God is able to take any circumstance and bring an *ultimate yes* out of it. When we are tied to the *initial nos* rather than the *ultimate yes*, it is usually because we have put conditions on God.

The pastor of a New Hampshire church we once attended told the story of two little French girls, Denise and Maria. Denise fell into a pond one day while the two were playing, and Maria managed to grab her long hair and hold her head above the water until help came. The press picked up the story of Maria's heroic gesture and came to interview her. How, they asked, had the incident changed her life? Her answer: "Denise won't play with me anymore; she says I pulled her hair."

So it seems that sometimes God is pulling our hair when, in fact, he is saving our lives. This concept can be appreciated only by an inner spirit looking for the *ultimate yes*.

Time to Reflect

With which of the people in these stories do you resonate? Think about whether you, like they, are looking for the yeses beyond the nos in your life. Write down any yeses that you have forgotten. Give thanks for them. What one step can you take toward the habit of seeking the yes rather than getting stuck in the no?

Prayer for the Day

Lord, I thank you for these people who have enlarged my thinking about how you work in our lives. Forgive me when I get stuck in the no and fear the future, thinking it's only a matter of time before "another shoe will fall." I want to be willing to go through the no so I can thank you for the yes.

Fifty-Six
છે.

Knowing Ourselves

Above all else, guard your heart, for it is the wellspring of
life.

PROVERBS 4:23

From the earliest days of my Christ-following life as a teen-
ager, I prayed for a heart that was sensitive to the needs of
others. In many ways, God has been kind to grant that request
to me. But there is a dimension to sensitivity that I have struggled with—being honest about and giving myself permission to
also have needs. Too often I have feigned strength, while feeling weak.

I had to face up to this many years ago when I watched our
daughter, Kristy, begin planning for college. At the time, she
was looking forward to rooming with a special friend. One
evening I commented to her, "You two won't even be homesick when you get to college; you're so close in your relationship."

"Yeah," Kristy responded. "You're right, Mom. We were saying that very thing the other day. No homesickness for us."
Ouch! Those seemingly innocent words cut deeply! But why
did they hurt? Should I have forgotten the pain and pressed on
with other things? Should I have simply told myself to grow up?
Be spiritual? Stop being a possessive mother?

No, it was a moment for me to be sensitive to myself, to look

185

at a truth within me. Hadn't I prayed regularly for our daughter to have such a friend? Yes, I had. Hadn't I known that eventually our second and last child would leave our nest? Of course. Then why was I consumed with such sadness when Kristy told me point-blank that she and her friend would make it just fine without their homes, without their mothers?

I left the room to get a grip on my feelings and thoughts. After acknowledging what I was feeling to myself, I returned. I decided it was time for an honest admission between us so that we could be even more genuine in the time to come.

To blend sensitivity to action, I had to weigh the two moods within me. On one hand the sadness of losing her, on the other hand, my joy over the anticipation bubbling inside of our daughter.

Kristy studied in her bedroom at her bedside. She would kneel with her papers spread all over her bed. In order to talk to her face-to-face, one had to "knee up" to the other side of the bed, so that's what I did.

"Kristy, it seems important that I tell you what I'm feeling right now—not only for my sake, but also for the years ahead when you go through these same things as a mother. I want you to know me not as a plastic, unfeeling, have-it-all-together person, but as one who struggles day after day to understand what's going on inside of her."

Kris listened, and I went on, "You know I've been praying for a friend for you who would understand and appreciate all that you are. Half of me is grateful for the answer to that prayer, but the other half of me grieves because I am slowly losing you. I know that I'm *not* losing you in actuality; but it feels like that."

At that, my eyes began to "leak," and instinctively Kristy reached out to gather me into her arms and said, "Oh, Mom, am I making it harder for you?"

"No, not at all," I responded. "This all needs to be. But I want you to know that I've never gone through releasing my last child before, and I may blow parts of the process. I hope you can help me by being patient and know that I'm trying to do it the best way I know how. Plus, I want you to never forget how grateful I am that you can make friends and plan a new world in which you are going to be more and more of what God wants you to become."

We two women—the younger and the older, the mother and the daughter—embraced in one of the tenderest moments of sensitivity that love can bring. She was safe in arms that are eternal. I would rest in that.

Time to Reflect

What do you do when you are walking through a situation similar to the one described here—cram your feelings or surface them in a safe place? Name the emotions this story brings out in you. Give thanks for times when you've been able to be authentic with someone you love, though it was possible they might not understand. Ask God for courage to be more and more honest with yourself and others.

Prayer for the Day

Lord, there are few things that mean more to me than a treasured experience like this. They are rare, but may come along more frequently than I choose to notice. Help me to seize opportunity for such intimacy with those I love so we can go deeper with each other, and you.

Fifty-Seven

Having True Comforters Alongside

Then Job replied, "I have heard many things like these; miserable comforters are you all! Will your long-winded speeches never end? What ails you that you keep on arguing? I also could speak like you, if you were in my place; I could make fine speeches against you and shake my head at you. But my mouth would encourage you; comfort from my lips would bring you relief."

JOB 16:1-5

One of the greatest lessons for us has been the importance of having friends close at hand with whom we have a reciprocal friendship where we and they can be healthy comforters when necessary.

We first discovered the role of the true comforter many years ago when our daughter Kristy, then two years old, accidentally drank some turpentine and was rushed to the hospital, gasping for air. Gordon and I had never felt so helpless. Being a pastor, Gordon had enjoyed unlimited access to the intensive care unit, but suddenly he was barred at the door, and both of us were restricted to five-minute visits every two hours. Inside that room we knew Kris was battling for her life. The doctors told us it would be twenty-four hours before they knew the outcome. The possibilities? Death, brain damage, kidney failure, or recovery.

Though that memory is more than thirty years old, both of

us vividly recall the men and women who came to sit with us. A prayer, an embrace, a cup of coffee, silence when necessary—they simply were *present* to us … no answers, no blaming, no explanations offered. They just came and gave us themselves.

God sent Ezekiel to a colony of Jewish exiles along the Chebar River in Babylon. "I went in bitterness and anger," Ezekiel recalled, "but the hand of the Lord was strong upon me. And I *sat among them, overwhelmed, for seven days*" (Ez 3:14-15, LB, emphasis mine). As Ezekiel sat with them, he was forced to feel what they felt, and his entire attitude was modified.

When Job's friends came to comfort him in his multiafflicted state, they were precisely what he seemed to need—for seven days. They were present to him. Alongside. Silent. But when they began to feel the horror of his pain and find that there seemed to be no "answers" for it, they became more of a nuisance than a comfort.

Finally, in a moment of utter frustration, feeling totally isolated, Job shouted at them, "Look at me" (Job 21:5), or, "Feel my pain. I'm a person just like you!"

Perhaps the reason Job got this strange kind of treatment from his friends was that he and his circumstances made the men feel insecure. How could they be sure that what he was experiencing wouldn't happen to them? Could they catch it, like the plague?

In that moment, they became less concerned with comforting Job and more interested in comforting themselves. What they were seeing upset their view of reality. If they got too close, their theology and their faith might be rocked by a situation that had no easy explanation. So, because of their fears, they ended up debating the origin and meaning of Job's problems rather than identifying with him as a person.

God, they said, wouldn't permit these things to happen to someone who was faithful and integral (like them). There! That settled it. "Now, Job," they seemed to say, "admit to us what you've done wrong [so we don't have to worry about this happening to us]."

This was no comfort, this was discomfort. Yet I see myself in their approach. Too many times, I, too, have tried to ease my own uneasiness about the unexplained nature of suffering, rather than quietly entering into another's grief and pain, *without needing to give answers.*

How good it is to have friends alongside who know what to do and not do in times of unexplained calamity.

Time to Reflect

Think back over conversations you have had with someone who was suffering. Have you cultivated friends who can be true comforter-friends? What stands out in their ability to listen and care for you? Have you told them the difference they have made? Can you also rejoice because you have been able to be a true comforter-friend to a few along the way?

Prayer for the Day

Father, I'm grateful for the Book of Job, Job's life, and what I can glean from it. Help me in this day to use care with people, to listen rather than offer opinions. May the grand ability of Jesus to look into the heart be manifested in me as I handle unexplainable dilemmas around me.

Fifty-Eight

The Rest of the Story

Let the word of Christ dwell in you richly as you teach and admonish one another with all wisdom, and as you sing psalms, *hymns and spiritual songs* with gratitude in your hearts to God.

COLOSSIANS 3:16, EMPHASIS MINE

I love offering praise and worship to God along with an enthusiastic congregation of people. The delicate balance of Scripture/praise songs mixed with the classic hymns never fails to lift my heart heavenward.

One Sunday, not long ago, a young woman I care for deeply was seated next to me in the sanctuary. We had just finished singing the hymn "It Is Well With My Soul," when she leaned over and said, "I don't enjoy singing hymns, but that one I love, because I know the story behind it."

Her comment, "I know the story behind it," created in me a desire to learn the stories behind the writing of many other hymns. Soon, I found myself becoming passionate about spreading the good news of what I discovered.

There are three hymn stories in previous sections, and they illustrate something important I learned: that an enormous percentage of great hymns have been written in the context of pain and suffering. Nevertheless, they brim with hope, with the conviction that God's faithfulness outweighs any challenge life can present. Great hymns reflect God's promises as they have been experienced by the hymn writer. Reading the stories of great hymns has powerfully changed me. For example, take the story behind the hymn "Children of the Heavenly Father."

Carolina (Lina) Sandell Berg was Sweden's greatest hymn writer. Born October 3, 1832, in Froderyd, Sweden, the daughter of a parish pastor, Berg became bedridden with a mysterious paralysis. Her doctors could do nothing for her and believed her case to be hopeless.

One Sunday morning, when she was twelve, her parents went to church and left Carolina at home so she could rest. She spent the time alone in prayer. When her parents came home, they were astonished to find her dressed and walking around the house! From that time on, she began to write, and in her sixteenth year, she published her first collection of hymns and poems.

Perhaps the best known of Carolina Berg's hymns is "Children of the Heavenly Father." Swedish Christians probably sing this hymn more than any other in the hymnal. In fact, my husband's grandfather died peacefully while his wife and eight children sang the many verses of this hymn into his heart. Some of them read:

> Children of the heav'nly Father
> Safely in His bosom gather;
> Nestling bird nor star in heaven
> Such a refuge e'er was given.

> God his own does tend and nourish,
> In his holy courts they flourish;
> From all evil things He spares them,
> In His mighty arms He bears them.

Neither life nor death shall ever
From the Lord His children sever;
Unto them His grace He showeth,
And their sorrows all He knoweth.[2]

I believe that it is of utmost importance that our grandchildren and their grandchildren know both hymns and spiritual songs. In times of desperation, we can be carried along and we can endure in strength if these truths have been musically imbedded in our hearts and minds. To let them slip away from us would be a great tragedy. Spread the joy. Pass the word.

Time to Reflect
Can you think of a hymn story that has made a hymn come alive to you? If you have found hymn singing a bore, is it time for you to choose to learn something new about hymnody so God can enlarge your heart toward him and his purposes? Perhaps checking a hymn-story book out of your church library would be a good place to begin.

Prayer for the Day
Lord, I admit to getting hung up on the old English in some hymns. Give me a renewed desire to find out how you have used music in the lives of your people throughout the generations. Change my heart, O God.

Fifty-Nine

Learning to Be a Comforter-Friend

The Spirit of the Lord is upon me; he has appointed me
to preach Good News to the poor; he has sent me to heal
the brokenhearted and to announce that captives shall be
released and the blind shall see, that the downtrodden
shall be freed from their oppressors, and that God is ready
to give blessings to all who come to him.

LUKE 4:18-19, LB

In this reading, Luke the physician wrote of how Jesus set the
direction of his earthly ministry by reading from Isaiah. If I
break out the verbs of that reading from all the other words, I
hear Jesus saying he came to comfort, rescue, release, and heal.
But should not these tasks belong to those who follow him as
well? Christ's dream seemed to be that succeeding generations
would do this task in an even greater and larger scope than he
did.

This kind of comforter-friend is never seen more clearly than
in Jesus' prediction of Simon Peter's denial on the night of the
Crucifixion. He warned Peter that he was going to fail, but did
not prevent his disciple from failing. That is important. While he
may not have wanted it to happen, *Jesus let Peter fail.*

The words that came next from Jesus were, "'Do not let your
hearts be troubled'" (Jn 14:1). I believe there is no coincidence
in this word placement. For Jesus was looking beyond the failure to the possibilities that would come afterward. He was

already looking toward the time of restoration when the lessons learned from the failure would be sorted out and welded into Peter's soul. Jesus, the Comforter-Friend, thought long term—before, during, and after the fall. Most of us do not.

One wonders how often in the years that followed, Peter looked back at that night when Jesus warned him of trouble and assured him that he was praying for him. It must have been a great lesson as to how much Jesus cared for him.

Not all of us are capable of being such a comforter-friend. The fact is that many of us don't know *how* to comfort. Some of us are afraid to try.

One day I asked a friend if, when her house burned to the ground, her friends were there for her. Some, yes, she said. Others, whom she thought were close friends, had avoided saying even one word to her. This "shunning" made things worse because it appeared that they were indifferent to her pain. In truth, they probably felt inadequate, not knowing what to say or do—they didn't have answers.

At such times, when comforting others is hard, we need to realize that a hug, a touch on the arm, a short prayer, or even a brief remark like, "I'm at a loss for words, but I care about you" helps immensely.

Each person's needs, how we express them, and how we wish to be comforted, all differ. I'm the kind who would like a few friends to walk *through* my dark times with me, but it's important to me that they not offer pity. I want them to challenge me to face the pain and encourage me to persevere.

I know others who prefer to keep their pain to themselves. In their anguish, they would like to be left alone. When you know such a person, you can only assure him or her that you're available and will check in from time to time and send notes to encourage instead. Yet, I have never met a person who didn't need the touches and prayers that reassure that there is life beyond these days of numbing limbo.

It's impressive that when Jesus was headed for the awful hours on the cross, he made no move to generate sympathy from the disciples. He *did*, however, want them close by: "Watch with me," and, "Pray with me."

The true comforter-friend comes alongside and offers himself as a companion in the pain or distress. Not a sermon. Not a cliché. Not an analysis. Not even an I-told-you-so. Just himself.

Time to Reflect

Think about those you love—what kind of comforter-friend do they need? Are there situations in your life right now that you've avoided because you've been unsure about how to be a comforter-friend? What step will you take toward confronting your fear or feelings of inadequacy?

Prayer for the Day

Thank you, Lord, that you model caring in such redeeming ways. Thank you that you look past the happy face to see the longing soul, the broken heart, the captive to addiction. I need to have *your* mind on these things. I admit to fear. I'm eager for your perfect love to overcome my fears so that I, too, can become one of your comforter-friends in motion.

sixty
ॐ

She's Not Disappointed

Look, I place in Zion a stone that will make people stumble, a rock that will make them fall. But whoever believes in him will not be disappointed.

ROMANS 9:33, GNB

I'll never forget the day I first heard Grace Fabian's testimony of how God's loving arms held her during the months following the murder of her husband of thirty-eight years.

Edmund and Grace Fabian went to Papua New Guinea in 1959 to translate the Scriptures into the Nabak language. The PNG, as it is called, became their home as they raised four children and devoted themselves to mastering the tribal tongues.

On April 29, 1993, Edmund was working alone with his language informant on a translation of 1 Corinthians 13, the famous love chapter, when his assistant suddenly picked up an ax and plunged it into his skull. Edmund died instantly. When interrogated, the assistant could say only that he had become tormented by voices in his head that compelled him to do violence.

Grace, who had been working in an adjacent room, was the first to find Edmund. The flashbacks she would have about that moment would go on for months and months. None of us can imagine the anguish of those first days of grief when Grace wondered if she could go on without Edmund's companionship and leadership. Thankfully, the closeness of their family drove them into even deeper intimacy.

Just before Edmund's death, he had been reading C.S. Lewis' book *Miracles*. Ironically, she had been reading a different book, entitled *When There Is No Miracle*. After his death, she was tempted to cry out, "Edmund, you got your miracle [being in the presence of Christ], but I didn't get mine."

She lamented to the Lord, "What should I do?" Even sitting in Edmund's office at the computer would bring painful memories, but she was practiced in going to God, and he began to bring important Scriptures to mind. Through those, he gave her a sense of his everlasting arms enveloping her at her point of greatest need.

First she was inspired by the story of Elisha (see 2 Kgs 6). The Syrian army had surrounded the city of Dothan with horses and chariots. Elisha's servant was terrified and asked the same question Grace was asking, "What shall we do?" (v. 15).

Elisha prayed, "O Lord, open his eyes so he may see" (v. 17). And when the Lord opened the servant's eyes, he saw the hills full of horses and chariots protecting Elisha. God's power was greater.

Then Grace looked at the parable of the talents (see Lk 19) and asked the question, "Why was the owner hard on the man with one talent?" The answer came back, "Because he didn't even *try*."

Grace then turned to her favorite, most often read prayer in the flyleaf of her Bible and let it percolate through her once more:

Lord, send me where you will
Only go with me.
Lay on me what you will
Only sustain me.
Cut any cord but the one that
Binds me to your Cause and your heart.

DAVID LIVINGSTONE

God's power was with her. She could do no less than try. The above verse from Romans had recently been translated—it became her very own. She would *not* be disappointed in her God…. The Nabak translation could be finished if she accepted God's power to help.

When each portion of the translation was completed, Grace took it to the jail and later the psychiatric ward where Edmund's assailant could take comfort in seeing it finished. Grace speaks freely of her joy in his being able to receive the forgiveness of God for killing Edmund. These are things God alone can do in us.

Finally the translation was completed. In September of 1998, there was a grand celebration. The Bible was presented to the Nabak people. There was even a reconciliation ceremony between the Fabian family and the clan of the man who killed Edmund. "We were inducted into their clan in a tear-filled ritual. We now have new sisters, brothers, aunts, and uncles."

Many of us would have lost our awareness of God's everlasting arms at such a time. But Grace said, "Death and sorrow will *not* have the last word. Not even an ax can separate us from the love of God." She had her miracle—a quiet inner strength, God's very own presence to give her the courage needed to pick up the task that seemed impossible and finish. And she did it while reaching out to the man who had killed her husband! One can live in this way only if yielded to *God's Everlasting Arms*. Grace says it forcefully, "I am not disappointed in my God."[28]

Time to Reflect

As these short devotionals come to an end, this story brings each section of the book together. What does Grace's testimony say to you? How will you choose to respond in the days ahead when hard things come your way? Do you now see the importance of searching the Scriptures for your comfort and direction? Or will you be satisfied with the opinions of people? Can you hold solidly to the knowledge that God's everlasting arms are there for you, no matter what?

Prayer for the Day

Lord, I'm awed by your work in this woman's life. Thank you for the way you have used this tragedy and others within this book to forge so much good for your kingdom. Please bring the heroes of faith like Grace to mind when I'm prone to wander or complain about the little things that go wrong in my life. I give myself to you, Lord Jesus. Thank you for taking me.

Notes

Section 1
A Look at the Heart of God

1. Amy Carmichael, *Rose from Brier* (Fort Washington, Pa.: Christian Literature Crusade, 1955), 151.
2. William Barclay, *Testament of Faith* (London and Oxford, England: Mowbrays, 1975), 46.
3. Joni Eareckson Tada, *Holiness in Hidden Places* (Nashville, Tenn.: Nelson, 1999), 69-70.
4. François Fénelon, *Spiritual Letters to Women* (Grand Rapids, Mich.: Zondervan, 1974), 264.
5. Oswald Chambers, *My Utmost for His Highest* (New York: Dodd, Mead and Co., 1954), 157.
6. Robert K. Brown and Mark R. Norton, *The One-Year Book of Hymns* (Wheaton, Ill.: Tyndale, 1995), September 26.
7. Carmichael, 19-20.
8. Harold Begbie, *The Life of General Booth, Vol. 1* (New York: Macmillan, 1920), 302.
9. Thomas à Kempis, *Of the Imitation of Christ, Selections* (Westwood, N.J.: Revell, 1963), 10.

Section 2
Making Pain Your Ally

1. Amy Carmichael, *Toward Jerusalem* (Fort Washington, Pa.: Christian Literature Crusade, 1936), 85.
2. Nicholas Wolterstorff, *Lament for a Son* (Grand Rapids, Mich.: Eerdmans, 1987), 89-90.
3. Brown and Norton, March 8.
4. Brown and Norton, March 8.
5. Michael Quoist, *Christ Is Alive* (New York: Doubleday, 1972), 86-87.
6. Brigid Hermann, *Creative Prayer* (Cincinnati, Ohio: Forward Movement), 39.
7. Amy Carmichael, *Edges of His Ways* (Fort Washington, Pa.: Christian Literature Crusade, 1955), 165.
8. Charles Spurgeon, *Streams in the Desert* (Grand Rapids, Mich.: Zondervan, 1965), 114.

9. C.W. Hall, *Samuel Logan Brengle: Portrait of a Prophet* (Chicago: Salvation Army, 1933), 89.

10. Pére Didon, as cited in Amy Carmichael, *Whispers of His Power* (Old Tappan, N.J.: Revell, 1982), 198-99.

Section 3
Courage to Find the High Road

1. Amy Carmichael, *Gold by Moonlight* (Fort Washington, Pa.: Christian Literature Crusade, 1951), 71.

2. Ruth Graham, *Ruth Bell Graham's Collected Poems, Footprints of a Pilgrim* (Grand Rapids, Mich.: Baker, 1998), 16.

3. Fénelon, 129.

4. Gigi Tchividjian, *Thank You, Lord, for My Home* (Minneapolis: World Wide: 1980), 96.

5. James D. Knowles, *Memoir of Ann H. Judson* (Boston: Gould, Kendall and Lincoln, 1849), 100.

6. Knowles, 174.

7. Morton Kelsey, *The Other Side of Silence* (Mahwah, N.J.: Paulist, 1976), 199.

8. E. Stanley Jones, *The Way* (New York: Abingdon-Cokesbury, 1946), 197.

9. Lloyd Ogilvie, *God's Best for My Life* (Eugene, Ore.: Harvest House, 1981), 8, 10, 15-16.

10. Brown and Norton, January 16.

11. Begbie, 289.

12. James Buchan, *The Expendable Mary Slessor* (New York: Seabury, 1981), 25.

Section 4
Pathways to Forgiveness

1. J. Danson Smith, *Springs in the Valley* (Grand Rapids, Mich.: Zondervan, 1938), 41.

2. John Perkins, *Let Justice Roll Down* (Ventura, Calif.: Regal, 1983), 205.

3. Phyllis Thompson, *D.E. Hoste* (London: Lutterworth, 1947), 121.

4. Bob Considine, "Could You Have Loved This Much?" *Reader's Digest*, April 1966, 73-75.

Section 5
Hitting Your Stride

1. Anne Morrow Lindbergh, *Gift From the Sea* (New York: Random, 1955), 57.
2. F.W. Boreham, *Shadows on the Wall* (London: Epworth, 1922), 44.
3. Fénelon, 16.
4. Edward England, *An Unfading Vision* (London: Hodder and Stoughton, 1982), 53.
5. David Lyle Jeffrey, *A Burning and a Shining Light* (Grand Rapids, Mich.: Eerdmans, 1987), 252-53.

Section 6
Living, Learning, and Passing It On

1. Sally Magnusson, *The Flying Scotsman* (Boston: Charles River, 1982), 37.
2. Brown and Norton, February 1.
3. Grace Fabian, *Through It All With Jesus, Story of Edmund and Grace Fabian,* Video produced by Wycliffe Bible Translators, 1998.